THE
INDIANAPOLIS
ANTHOLOGY

MORE CITY ANTHOLOGIES FROM BELT

The Dayton Anthology

The Louisville Anthology

The Gary Anthology

Car Bombs to Cookie Tables: The Youngstown Anthology, Second Edition

The Columbus Anthology

The St. Louis Anthology

Under Purple Skies: The Minneapolis Anthology

The Milwaukee Anthology

Rust Belt Chicago: An Anthology

Grand Rapids Grassroots: An Anthology

Happy Anyway: A Flint Anthology

The Akron Anthology

Right Here, Right Now: The Buffalo Anthology

The Cleveland Anthology, Second Edition

The Pittsburgh Anthology

A Detroit Anthology

The Cincinnati Anthology

THE
INDIANAPOLIS
ANTHOLOGY

EDITED BY **NORMAN MINNICK**

Belt Publishing

First Edition 2021
ISBN: 978-1-948742-91-7

Belt Publishing
5322 Fleet Avenue, Cleveland, OH 44105
www.beltpublishing.com

Book design by Meredith Pangrace
Cover by David Wilson

Dedicated in memory of

Mari Evans (1919–2017)
Jim Powell (1950–2020)

devoted advocates for writing and community

CONTENTS

Introduction: Indianoplace; Or, What Results from Being Plunked down on a Flat, Swampy, Heavily Forested Tract of Land
Norman Minnick .... page 13

Home
Allyson Horton .... page 17

Our House
Barbara Shoup .... page 19

Back Home Again in Indy
Jared Carter .... page 23

International Oasis in the Midwest
Desiree Arce.. page 24

State Museum Thoughts
Sandy Eisenberg Sasso .... page 27

Permission on Holy Ground
Chantel Massey.. page 28

Find Your Own
Bryan Furuness.. page 30

Doc Coe and the Malaria Epidemic
Nelson Price .... page 31

Indianapolis
Kaitlynne Mantooth.. page 33

Tibbs Drive-In
Anne Laker .... page 37

Indy 500, 1975
Grant Vecera.. page 38

Hawking Indy 500 Souvenirs during the 100th Running of the Greatest Spectacle in Racing
Michael Brockley .... page 39

This Is Dogtown
Nasreen Khan..page 40

Jim Jones Goes to Night School
Nate Logan ....page 42

Punk Rock in Naptown
Stephanie Reid..page 43

East Side
Jackie Lutzke..page 44

Indianapolis
Fran Quinn ....page 46

Imagining the Black Crossroads:
Music and Memory on Indiana Avenue
Paul R. Mullins and Jordan B. Ryan......................page 47

Red Clay
Chris Speckman...page 62

Leaving Indiana after X-Mas, 1987
Etheridge Knight ....page 64

Busking on State Capital Streets
Norbert Krapf...page 66

What Was the Contribution of Neighbors?
Terrance Hayes ....page 67

My Father's Keeper
Ashley Mack-Jackson..page 70

In Indy, #BLACKYOUTHMATTER!
Darolyn "Lyn" Jones...page 72

How an Old White Guy Got Woke
Dan Wakefield...page 74

Reclamation
Sarah Layden ....page 83

CONTENTS

Transpo
Theon Lee..page 85

Fountain Fossil
Manòn Voice ....page 87

Growing Food in the City: Urban Agriculture
and Community Gardens in Indianapolis
Angela Herrmann...page 89

Eight Gardens: On Gardening as Social Practice
Kevin McKelvey...page 97

Mama's Back Porch on Dorman St.
Izera McAfee ....page 104

Walking to the Circle: 25 Miles through a
Divided City
Michael McColly..page 105

Icons from Indianapolis
Ruth Stone ....page 113

Miss Victory (1895)
Karen Kovacik...page 114

Monument Circle
Elizabeth Krajeck ....page 115

Soldiers and Sailors Monument, Indianapolis
Dan Grossman ....page 116

Downtown, Anywhere
Malachi Carter...page 117

Wild in Indianapolis
Lylanne Musselman ....page 119

In Sight It Must Be Right
Michael Martone...page 120

Jazz Kitchen
Nick Reading .... page 122

Floral Lady's Employer Files for Bankruptcy
Natalie Solmer .... page 123

Requiem of a Womanist Library Trustee
Dr. Terri Jett .... page 125

**"Moral Warfare": Indianapolis Women's
Long-Fought Battle for the Vote**
Nicole Poletika .... page 131

Sarah's Exodus
Shari Wagner .... page 139

**The Story behind Telling
Madam C. J. Walker's Story,**
A'Lelia Bundles .... page 141

Pink Poodle
Will Higgins .... page 144

Birds of Prey
Susan Neville .... page 150

Puppies 4 Sale
Jim Powell .... page 162

Ruth Lilly's House
Norman Minnick .... page 167

Mourning at the MLK-RFK Memorial
Dan Carpenter .... page 168

Through Our Eyes
Tatjana Rebelle .... page 171

Contributors .... page 173
Permissions .... page 185

INDIANOPLACE; OR, WHAT RESULTS FROM BEING PLUNKED DOWN ON A FLAT, SWAMPY, HEAVILY FORESTED TRACT OF LAND

NORMAN MINNICK

"You can make something out of nothing in Indianapolis."
—Zero Boys

"Are you still in basketball-crazed Indianoplace?"

This gem was made by none other than Hillary Rodham Clinton in an email to an aide in 2010. "It was a joke," Clinton later claimed. "I know even people in Indiana make that joke."

Isn't she Hillarious? Allow me to break this down.

1. According to Urban Dictionary, this derogatory name for Indianapolis "comes from the evident lack of anything to do other than get drunk and watch sports and the appearant [sic] resistance of many of its inhabitants to allow culture, change, or diversity into the mix." While getting drunk and watching sports is indeed a pastime in Indianapolis, it isn't a result of "the evident lack of anything to do." And, while many of its inhabitants are resistant to allowing culture, change, or diversity into the mix, culture, change, and diversity are definitely in the mix in Indianapolis.

2. Indiana may be known as a basketball-crazed state, but it isn't. Maybe in its heyday when throwing chairs across the court was fashionable, but I can tell you, being a basketball fan from Kentucky, I was flummoxed when I moved here by just how few people are crazy about the sport.

3. Hillary Clinton may be known for her scintillating one-liners such as, "I don't know who created Pokémon Go, but I'm trying to figure out how to get them to have Pokémon-go-to-the-polls" or "By the way, you may have seen that I recently launched a Snapchat account.... Those

messages disappear all by themselves," but let's face it, Sasheer Zamata she is not.

4. Only Hoosiers can make this joke.

But to say that "Indianapolis has no reason to exist," that's another topic for debate. This bon mot opens Joseph S. Pete's literary tour of Indianapolis in the magazine *Thoughtful Dog*. He notes, "Most American cities grew organically by harbors, river oxbows, and Great Lakes—assembling around ports that made them hubs of commerce and connected them to the wider world. Indianapolis was plunked down on a flat, swampy, heavily forested tract of land to serve as a state capital."

It is, perhaps, the flat terrain and unnavigable river that adds to Indianapolis's mystique as a dull, monotonous city lacking culture, change, or diversity. Even its famed racecourse is flat and, according to *Bleacher Report,* the Indianapolis Motor Speedway is second only to Pocono Raceway as the least exciting racecourses in the country.

Its landscape is as flat as a basketball court. This is a lie, of course. The highest point in Indianapolis is in Crown Hill Cemetery at the tomb of famed Hoosier writer James Whitcomb Riley. Anyone from Indianapolis will tell you this. It is also a lie.

What do you call someone from Indianapolis, anyway? "Hoosier" is more of a rural thing. It evokes images of rusted basketball hoops drooping from the sides of barns surrounded by acres of corn. I've heard suggested "Indianapolitans," which I rather like. But "Nap-towners" wins the day. Not only does it cleverly make use of a play on words better than "Indianoplace," but the 'n' and 'p' and 'ow' sounds lend themselves to the quintessential Midwest nasal accent "where common speech sounds like a band saw cutting galvanized tin and employs a vocabulary as un-ornamental as a monkey wrench." This may offend some, but Kurt Vonnegut said it, so it's okay.

Kurt Vonnegut is, of course, from Indianapolis and is known for his dark humor and his novels *Slaughterhouse-Five, Cat's Cradle,* and my favorite, *Breakfast of Champions.* We like to quote him a lot. "All my jokes are Indianapolis. All my attitudes are Indianapolis. My adenoids are Indianapolis." —Kurt Vonnegut.

You know who else is from Indianapolis? Kenneth "Babyface" Edmonds, David Letterman, Steve McQueen (the actor; not the director), Steve Ells, founder and CEO of Chipotle Mexican Grill, and "Black Doug" from *The Hangover.* But they don't have murals in the city. You know does? Kurt Vonnegut. There is also a mural of the late Mari Evans, a leading poet of the Black Arts Movement and one of the most influential Black poets of the twentieth century. Although she was celebrated more outside the city she called home, she did more for the people of Indianapolis, especially youth in urban communities, than any poet I have ever known.

The poet Etheridge Knight also did a great deal for his community. He led Free People's Poetry Workshops, which were free and open to anyone who wished to attend. He does noes not have a mural. Neither does Freddie Hubbard, J. J. Johnson, Wes Montgomery, or Albert Von Tilzer, whose song "Take Me Out to the Ballgame" is sung countless times each summer in baseball parks across the United States.

Marguerite Young doesn't have a mural either. Her 1965 novel *Miss MacIntosh, My Darling* was considered by the *New York Times Book Review* to be "a work of stunning magnitude and beauty... in the great styles of Joyce or Broch or Melville or Faulkner." It is also one of the longest novels ever written; longer than *Les Misérables* or *War and Peace*.

In her *Paris Review* interview, Young said, "I was born in Indianapolis, Indiana, 'the Athens of the West,' as it had been called in an earlier day. That was when Booth Tarkington, Meredith Nicholson, James Whitcomb Riley, various writers of the old Hoosier group lived there. We were brought up to believe that to be born in Indiana was to be born a poet."

As a poet, when I see the word used in this context, I think not just of people who write poems but anyone possessing unique powers of imagination or expression such as those listed above and those in the book you hold in your hands. Here is a taste of what you will find in the following pages: lawn chairs in the beds of pick-ups; front porches; pool memories and hot pavement; jazz and blues; classical; punk rock; railroads and breakneck highways; the magnificent stench of diesel, sweat, and sweetly hissing charcoal; limestone; grocery stores; suffragists and entrepreneurs; cement Pietàs; cicadas; popcorn; kites in trees; mixtapes and thrills; sneakers dangling from power lines; prom corsages and teens with frohawks; community gardens; soybeans and hog reports; Jim Nabors' greatest hits; perpetual road construction; city busses; hook-up hotels; dog bakeries and yoga studios; red brick bungalows and war memorials; steakburgers and Mexican seafood; Vietnamese pho and sauerbraten; shade tree mechanics; lots of bars and churches; drive-ins; racecars; mosquitos; drag shows and cocktail lounges; Shakespearean theatre; jokes that are not funny. And some that are.

What makes Indianapolis Indianapolis is in the nuances. Hopefully, this book serves as a *vade mecum* of sorts for Nap-towners and visitors alike so that no one feels like Lawrence Ferlinghetti in his poem "Don't Cry for Me Indiana," as if they "just got beamed down by Scotty in *Star Trek /* What is this place…?" I heard Ferlinghetti read a draft of this poem the day after he composed it when he read to a packed house at Clowes Memorial Hall on Butler University's campus. As he autographed my book, I made the feeble attempt to make an impression on the great poet with an old chestnut: "Welcome to Indianoplace."

HOME

ALLYSON HORTON

is where the wheat is

       the sweet is of yellow corn
the vastness of virile plains
plunge & plow of tractors grinding
through thick soil: glacial sands, gravel, clay
producing fertile rows of fragrant harvest
signature as a Midwest skyline.
Home
is where the stretch of long road
smiles & smiles for emerald miles
where an abundance of local crops
choir crisp hymns in the rustic breeze   gently chant
praises of cha-ching   spit tufts of dirt
in the wind all eyes & ears pointing
toward the trough of bastard children
threatening to change the landscape
validating the question—Hoosier Daddy?
Yes, home of the jokes
that aren't funny   like Indiananoplace.
Like a baseball league of Negro
men labeled Indianapolis Clowns.
Like a reservation of sacred mounds
of charred Redskins belonging to Natives & Chiefs
whose roots be thicker than indigenous
lines drawn between wigwams & tepees.
Buried narratives idiomatic as Indian-ah.
Home
is where we have yet to reap all that has been sown
in the scalps of ancient memory
& on tongues of sun-dried bodies
dangling from blood-smudged photos
polaroiding klansmen, women
& owl-eyed offspring

learning the ropes.
Home
is where cross the tracks my parents
were educating me about ropes.
Today, I travel light when roaming
these historic parts of my beloved state   like Martinsville
where a Black female student en route to IU
can still stand face to face with sundown
signs: warning shots alerting my kind
that I's gon be need'n to hightail it, after dark
making Indiana
home of the "good lookin out" incentives.
Home of an ongoing campaign
to promote "reading" among minority youth
& home of the introduction on how to decipher
20th century American "sign" language,
but I have since learned how to burrow through
blurred perimeters   small-minded geography
where luminous night star & crossroads burn
clear. Tracking footprints of refugee
sharecroppers has landed me here
where I, too, have decided to plant my feet
in the heart of the capital's sky-scraping potential
so when one of my girlfriends living in D.C.
asks why I continue to relate to "such a conservative
state like Indiana" as Home
I simply tell her—border for border
it is the only place I trust.

OUR HOUSE

BARBARA SHOUP

I was twenty-one, two years married, and the mother of an eighteen-month-old daughter when my husband graduated from Indiana University and took a job in Indianapolis. We needed a house, his parents decided, and they would provide the down payment. There was no joy in it: an early marriage and a too-soon baby were not what they had envisioned for their only son. That and my mother-in-law's grim Lutheran sensibility ensured the house wouldn't be anything fancy.

My dream house: a two-story white colonial with shutters, bay windows, a fireplace, window seats in the bedrooms, a screened-in porch, and an attic—preferably surrounded by a white picket fence. In an old neighborhood.

The house my mother-in-law chose for us: a single-story red brick bungalow with rough limestone trim around the door, a cement front porch, ugly steel casement windows, prickly plaster on the walls, no woodwork, and ghastly pink and blue glass tile in the bathroom. It was in an old neighborhood, a couple of blocks north and east of a *really* nice old neighborhood.

We won't live here forever, I told myself.

That was 1969.

A big maple tree stood on one side of the front sidewalk when we moved into 6012 North Broadway, and a redbud on the other. The park across the street, lined with maple trees, had swings, a tall silver slide, and a merry-go-round made of a flat circle of steel with bars to hold onto. Around it, a trench had been worn in the ground by running feet. There was a concrete spray pool surrounded by a cyclone fence, as well as two tennis courts and a basketball court. An Indianapolis Park Department employee kept the grass cut and the bushes groomed, and college girls were hired to organize activities for the neighborhood kids and supervise the spray pool in the summer.

Binkley's Drugstore, complete with soda fountain, was just around the corner on College Avenue and across the street from it, a small family grocery store. You could walk a couple of blocks north to feed the ducks on the canal, and then a few more blocks east to Broad Ripple Village, which was like a small town, with an elementary school, a post office, a fire station, a movie theater, a dime store, a stationery store, a dress shop, a florist, a kosher deli, and an ice cream parlor.

Downtown was a twenty-minute drive if you hit the lights just right.

Time goes by. I finished my college degree a few classes at a time. My husband went to law school nights, working a full-time day job. We had a second daughter the year he graduated, and our older daughter started kindergarten at School 80 not long after that. A few years later I started teaching, which I loved.

We'd talk about moving, but the houses we could afford were in the suburbs, the very idea of which I'd loathed since childhood, when my family moved from a city neighborhood to one of those cookie-cutter post-WW2 subdivisions in the middle of nowhere. Plus, we loved our Broad Ripple neighborhood and its mix of people. An elderly couple lived in the double next door; across the street, a family with three grown daughters, our age, and a younger one who soon became our beloved babysitter. A few families on the block had kids the same age as our daughters, others had middle school kids who zoomed around on bikes, or teenage kids who hung out in the park with their friends, sometimes late into the night. A nutty lady who delighted in conspiracy theories lived on the corner; a retired French professor bounced by most days on his constitutional walk; what we came to think of as the Dog Club gathered with their morning coffees or evening beers to give their dogs a run in the park.

We got the bug for skiing, bought a drafty orange VW van—and headed for Michigan most winter weekends, eventually buying a small house near a ski area. I took my much longed for first trip to Europe and wanted more. My husband loved cars and motorcycles; enough said about that. Our kids were settled in their schools, happy with their neighborhood pals.

I still wanted that damn house, though. *A lot.* And we might have been able to afford it by then, but it would have meant not doing things we loved to do, not having things that seemed crucial to who we were. Even so, we might have had it if I hadn't finally gathered up my courage to write—and to be the writer I wanted and needed to be meant a part-time job.

Writing vs. Dream House. It wasn't really a choice for me. I wrote.

Who knew? Maybe I'd publish a best-selling novel and I could have it all. That did not happen.

Meanwhile, we celebrated everything from birthdays to graduations, engagements, weddings, and babies on the way in our house. We established amusing traditions, such as the annual Turkey Trot we hosted every Thanksgiving for years with its costumed runners, front porch pageant, and blessing of the shoes. And our Christmas (and other special occasion) Waffle Toss, in which family members toss leftover waffles like Frisbees, attempting to get them into the front window of one of our cars. We stood outside on Friday nights in the fall and listened to the Broad Ripple High School band playing a few blocks away and on Sunday mornings when we could hear church bells ringing.

Whoosh! In what felt like a Chutes and Ladders move, it was 2020.

––––––––––

The maple trees lining the park are gone now, replaced by flowering pears that burst into beautiful, but stinky white blooms in the spring. The playground equipment is kid-safe, the spray pool redesigned, the basketball goal replaced by a volleyball court where an LGBTQ group flies a rainbow flag most Sunday afternoons. The tennis courts are blue instead of the traditional green. Every spring, the entire student body of School 84 marches to the park wearing tie-dye shirts for their Peace Day celebration, where they sing and play ukuleles.

Binkley's Drug Store became Binkley's Kitchen and Bar, great for a quick burger after a long day; the little grocery store was divided into Ambrosia, a high-end Italian restaurant, and Haus Love, featuring expensive home décor. You can still find ducks along the canal, though some of the towpath has been paved for walkers and bikers. The post office and fire station remain in Broad Ripple Village, but the village itself has become a party destination for college kids and millennials. In addition to its many bars and restaurants, there's a Starbucks, a dog bakery, a tattoo parlor, as well as galleries, artsy shops, and yoga studios. The elementary school has been turned into condos where alums have the option to live in their favorite classroom.

You can still get downtown in twenty minutes if you hit the lights just right, but traffic and perpetual road construction make it less likely that you'll accomplish it. Or you could hop on your bike and take the Monon Trail, which runs through Broad Ripple Village all the way to Massachusetts Avenue.

———————

Our house is still far from fancy, but over the years it's morphed into, well, *ours*. We replaced the ugly steel casement windows, painted the porch brick-red, and installed a striped awning, which in the warm weather shelters white wicker furniture and pots of ferns and flowers. In the seventies, we built an addition that stretches along the back of the house and opens into a cloistered garden.

The pink and blue tiles in the bathroom are gone, the kitchen remodeled. The rooms are painted warm, cozy colors and hung with art posters I've collected over the years. There are bookshelves groaning with books, and comfy chairs and couches for reading nearly everywhere you look. Antiques, family photos, plants, flea market treasures, and quirky travel mementos make it a house no decorator could have designed.

The elderly couple who lived next door in 1967 were in their seventies.

We're the elderly next-door neighbors in their seventies now.

———————

It is at the same time lovely and melancholy to stay in the same place for more than fifty years. The ghosts of our little girls live in this house, in this neighborhood, along with the ghosts of our younger selves—and the younger selves of family and friends. Memories are more vivid, I think, remembered where they happened; more visceral, confined to their original space—and interestingly, if maddeningly, tangled with years of other memories formed in that exact spot.

I had to laugh when the Broad Ripple Village Association asked to include our house in its 2014 home tour. My first thought was: *I always wanted a house worthy of a house tour but forgot to tell the cosmos that I wanted that house to be the house of my dreams.*

The thing is, I still want it.

I always will, despite recognizing the longing as residue of a childhood belief that the bigger and nicer the house, the happier the family. But when house angst pays its regular calls, I ask myself: *Who would you be if you didn't live here?* And I don't really want to know the answer.

BACK HOME AGAIN IN INDY

JARED CARTER

Full-bird colonel, Army Infantry,
Airborne Ranger, served thirty years
abroad, stationed in Kosovo, Iceland,
Germany, Greece, Ft. Leavenworth.
A friend, a former student of mine,
he recently retired, and decided
to look me up. We are having lunch
in a pleasant downtown restaurant
specializing in German cuisine.
He says now that Indy is home,
he's looking to buy a house.
"My realtor has this list," he says.
"In the first house he showed me,
there were bones everywhere."
"Bones? What kind of bones?"
"All kinds," he says, "Skeletons.
Human, animal. Horse. Dog."
"Just laying around?" "Right.
Evidently the previous owner
had moved out but didn't take
his bone collection with him."
For a moment I concentrate
on my potato pancake, which
is excellent. "It seemed like
a bad sign," he adds, halfway
through his *Sauerbraten*.
"But of course I've lived in
some pretty strange places."
"Welcome to Indianapolis," I say.

INTERNATIONAL OASIS IN THE MIDWEST

DESIREE ARCE

I moved to Indianapolis almost ten years ago. I learned very quickly how warm and welcoming Hoosiers could be, despite the fact they rarely kiss, something very common in Argentina. When spring arrived, I noticed something that everybody seemed to ignore: Indiana's wonderful trees. Everything started turning green and colorful around the suburban areas. I could barely keep track of the different parks we had visited, and I wanted to visit them all; so many trees, so much nature.

However, after a while, I realized something was quite not right. I was in the United States, the land of immigrants, but I have barely seen any. I started to believe that there weren't many people like me in Indianapolis.

Everything changed when I started working near the Indianapolis Motor Speedway, which is, by the way, the most iconic reference someone could give for Indianapolis. Soon I learned there was a *New York Times* article dedicated to describing the particularities of a place where people could find restaurants from all around the world. My mind was blown by the fact that I had just discovered a secret place (at least for me) where Indianapolis hid its magnificent global diversity, the Indianapolis International Marketplace. If you look carefully, you can see some signs announcing you are entering a different place between 46th Street and Lafayette Road (North) and 34th Street and Lafayette Road (South). After many years working in the area, I get to explore and know so many cool places, restaurants, grocery stores, and people that I couldn't even describe in a few pages. Yet I feel obligated to at least enumerate what I consider some of its landmarks.

The Saraga International Grocery is an international oasis in the middle of the Midwest. The name itself means lovely, charming, or strong in Sanskrit, which describes what, for a lot of people, is almost an adventure. From the moment you enter the main doors, you can immediately observe unidentifiable produce. Weirdly shaped vegetables, exotic fruits and a lot of things you'll need to Google. The meat department offers an extended array of seafood products including live lobsters, sea urchins, octopus, and other exotic water creatures. Every department will strike you with the same amount of surprise. They have so many different and particular products that the aisles are divided into regions: Asia, Africa, South America, Central America, etc. One of my favorites is their tea selection, with varieties from all around the world and any ingredients you can think of. They also have some subleased restaurants inside the store: a Chinese one, a taqueria, a halal butchery, and a bakery, in that order. At the checkout line, I notice myself among people from different ethnicities, overhearing three or four different languages, each of us paying for our precious cultural necessities.

Another landmark supermarket is the Carnicería Guanajuato, which serves as a cheap trip to Mexico for locals. Once you enter the grocery store you can immediately notice that Spanish becomes the primary language. Their bakery department is always a temptation. You won't find any products that aren't from Mexico or another Central American country. And if you become hungry after seeing all those tacos, burritos, and enchilada ingredients, there is also a restaurant attached where you can taste everything you saw earlier. The atmosphere makes you feel like you are seated in a real Mexican patio. Their "tablas" serve as great catering for special events too.

Pertaining to restaurants, whether you want to try some of the most authentic Mexican seafood in town while singing karaoke like at El Puerto de San Blas or try some of the best Vietnamese pho's (my favorite is the chicken cashew) at King Wok or stop for a delicious tandoori fried chicken at Shani's Secret Chicken, you have hundreds of flavors from all around the world in only 2.5-mile area. No need to bring a passport.

Although the architecture belies its history as any other neighborhood in the city, the Indianapolis International Marketplace has become unlike any other place. It almost feels like you are somewhere else and nowhere at the same time. Little I knew when I first moved to Indianapolis that a place in the Midwest would hold such cultural diversity.

Indiana is known as the Crossroads of America but at the Indianapolis International Marketplace, it has also become the crossroads of the world.

STATE MUSEUM THOUGHTS

SANDY EISENBERG SASSO

This is an address upon receiving the Heritage Keeper Award at the Indiana State Museum, 2014. The award is given to "Indiana's greatest ambassadors for their embodiment of the Hoosier spirit in their accomplishments, leadership, and service to the state." —Ed.

There is a story that speaks of the creation of the world. After the six days of fashioning land and sea, the plants, the fish that swim in the sea, the animals that fly in the sky and the ones that walk on the ground—and finally, man and woman created in the divine image, the angels ask God, "Is the world finished yet?" And God answers, "I don't know, go ask my partners!"

This Museum showcases the artifacts of those partners, indelible marks left in time, a living history with a continuing presence. By seeing what was, the choices made, we can better imagine what may yet become. Indiana is the place of our memories, those we have inherited and those we are creating, that allow us to call Indiana our home.

When Dennis and I crossed the state line as we moved from New York to Indianapolis in 1977 to begin our rabbinical calling at Beth-El Zedeck, we listened to the local radio station. Someone was giving the soybean and hog report. I thought to myself, "Where in the world are we going? Could Indiana ever become the place of our memories? Could we ever call Indiana home?"

My friends from the East would tell me about a new East Coast trend and conclude with the remark, "Well, you wouldn't know about that. It probably hasn't made it to Indiana."

I soon discovered that lots of things did make it to Indiana—from best-selling authors and poets to painters and musicians, from symphony to the theatre, from universities to museums, from vice presidents to astronauts, from a strong public square to philanthropy.

Many slogans have been used to define Indiana—from "Crossroads of America" to "Honest to Goodness." I'd like to suggest another slogan: "Be Surprised." That is what I have been.

Our state environment was once ripe for mammoths, bison, and bears. Over time the soil supported hardwood forests, limestone quarries, factories, and farms.

Indianapolis was once swamp and marshland. When the capital was built here, devastating malarial fever claimed many lives. But the swamp gave way to a city. Now when you say Indiana Fever, you are referring to a championship WNBA team.

Some of what found a home in Indiana, we recall with regret. The Ku Klux Klan dominated state and city government in the 1920s. The John Birch Society was established here in 1958. The old Riverside Amusement Park restricted attendance by Blacks to designated days for 50 years. Now in the very location of that park is the Velodrome, named after Major Taylor, a world champion bicyclist who was African American.

There is much we remember with Hoosier pride. From 1900-1920 Indiana ranked second among the states in best-selling books. We experienced a golden age—politically and economically. Culture flourished, producing nationally known musical composers and the Hoosier Group of landscape painters. The Circle Theater was once a silent movie house. Some of the musicians who accompanied the movies were among the core group who helped to found our world-class Indianapolis Symphony.

Since Dennis and I arrived in Indiana we have witnessed an increasing diversity of language, religion, ethnicity, and a renewal of urban life. We are nearing our state bicentennial. We've traveled from mammoths to monuments, from Ku Klux Klan to cultural trail, from insularity to greater inclusivity. Some events and people come easily to mind, but there are stories that remain hidden. We need acts of willed remembrance to ensure that those stories are told. We bring to mind failures and triumphs in order to respond to present challenges and guide our future to make this a state of abundant opportunity for all its citizens.

It is human imagination that gives meaning to time. Seasons come and go, but we are the ones who divide months into weeks, the year into sacred moments and years into historical ages and epochs. The physicist and writer Alan Lightman reminds us, "We come and go quickly; we want something to last." As we move forward, the question is: what of ourselves do we want to last, what environment do we want to create, what do we want Hoosier to mean?

Our son was one year old when Dennis and I came here in 1977. Our daughter was born at Methodist Hospital. We are now proud to call ourselves Hoosiers; this is the place of our memories and our future. Now I can answer my own question, "Where in the world are we going?" We are going home.

PERMISSION ON HOLY GROUND

CHANTEL MASSEY

at the bottom of a glass of Jose Cuervo
is the burning bush i am Moses
my tongue a fish, my mouth a bowl
it breaks open and out cries an aching laugh

by shot 2 with sweat on my chest
watch my body branch
into a church
into a celebration.

by shot 2, my feet know the middle of streets
are holy ground so i dance on yellow lines
my knees bent /my feet step / my gap out
like this is the first time i have ever arrived

like
like its 1992
Afro-beat bang in the street
on Mass ave. and i dance

my homegirl chants *AYE* with her phone on me:
Black body in the middle of the street that is warm
and *moving*. my locs sway on my face
i can feel my laugh—like a choir hum

of bees swell from my chest
i sing and out comes the smoke
i swallowed the fire
let it be known that on this day,

i have been reborn at least three times
by now, this was the third
as the car lights orbit *this* body of a planet—
i mean is it not otherworldly to watch a Black girl like this?

watch her beam?
watch her bend into an eclipse?
drivers thought the moon sunk into itself.
it did. along with everything else

consumed by
the riot
in my dance
in my joy
in my hands
i ask
—is this not a riot?

FIND YOUR OWN

BRYAN FURUNESS

At twenty-three, I worked in advertising for the *Indianapolis Star*. Not a bad job, but I was desperate to leave. I wanted to do something with books, something with words. During the summer I started taking my lunch break at the Central Library. I'd eat a sandwich on the walk there and read for the rest of the hour. After a few visits, I settled on a favorite spot: a heavy wooden table on the second floor, flanked by walls of books, with one high leaded window letting in some watery light. Secluded, silent, cool, dim: what a find.

One day—this might have been in the third week of my routine—a man shuffled up to the table. He was wrapped in a quilted blanket. I tried to focus on my book, but this became impossible when he opened the blanket like a bat spreading its wings. Still, I might have recovered my concentration if the man hadn't been naked.

Or if the funk, released from the blanket like a smoke signal, hadn't been so eye-watering.

Or if he hadn't proceeded to parade around the table three times, majestically, holding the blanket wide open.

Actually, the man might have gone around that table more than three times, I don't know. By his second lap, I was packing up to leave.

Now, years later, I'm thinking about the solemn way he walked around the table. Like some kind of ritual, but for what?

Maybe this was his special spot. Maybe he was exorcising me.

None of this occurred to me at the time. I was twenty-three, trying to carve out a space of my own in the world. It didn't occur to me that at this late date, all the best spots were taken.

DOC COE AND THE MALARIA EPIDEMIC

NELSON PRICE

Indianapolis Almost Died Before Beginning

No one remembers Doc Coe, much less celebrates him. The site of his wood-frame home and doctor's office on Monument Circle has been occupied since 1925 by the ritzy Columbia Club, the private gathering place for movers and shakers.

Not only has Dr. Isaac Coe been long forgotten, so has the malaria epidemic of 1821 that almost wiped out the brand-new city of Indianapolis just as the earliest white settlers were arriving in the marshland planned as the state's capital city. The only surviving clue is about one mile away, a plaque at Indiana University-Purdue University at Indianapolis. The plaque honors pioneers buried in obscure "Plague Cemetery," the city's first public graveyard.

You could make a case the fledgling city might have died along with those pioneers if not for Doc Coe, a New Jersey native who became the second physician to show up in the wilderness town. His arrival in May of 1821 preceded a humid, mosquito-infested summer and the beginnings of the malaria misery. According to some accounts, nearly one-eighth of Indianapolis's population died during the devastating epidemic. Dozens of other residents, terrified by the "plague," packed up and left. Many wondered whether this new city would endure.

"You fools," Doc Coe scolded state leaders. He chastised them for selecting a miserable site for the new capital city, genuflecting to surveyors merely because they had determined it was the geographic center of the nineteenth state. Swamps and marshlands here were causing the malaria, according to Doc Coe, who blamed their "vapors." Physicians in the twenty-first century have more complex, nuanced explanations, but say Doc Coe was on the right track—almost a medical visionary—in attributing much of the epidemic to the ill-advised, swampy site.

For those resilient residents who remained, Doc Coe became a folk hero. From his house on Monument Circle—a dirt road known then as "Circle Street"—the pioneer doctor worked nearly to the point of exhaustion, tending to his neighbors' chills, fevers, and other symptoms of the epidemic. Until Doc Coe died in 1855, his neighbors on Circle Street were private houses and churches. Except for the eternal Christ Church Episcopal Cathedral, none of those structures remain.

Doc Coe may have been a savior, but he wasn't a saint. He became a fierce advocate for something else ill-advised: the canal system that would essentially bankrupt the state. There even were accusations Doc Coe was involved in financial irregularities connected to the canals.

The city has endured despite the malaria, the canal fiasco—and different, stifling challenges during the late 1960s and 1970s when I was growing up and my dad's law office was located in the Circle Tower Building, the Art Deco structure on Monument Circle just a stethoscope's throw from where Doc Coe's office stood.

That era was the nadir of "Naptown" when even the second oldest structure on Monument Circle (after Christ Church Cathedral) slid into inglorious decay. Built in 1916 as a lavish movie palace, the Circle Theatre was showing a third-run film on a cracked screen when, as adolescents, my best friend and I sneaked in after visiting Dad's office. The Circle Theatre's sharply inclined floor was carpeted with vermin, although not the mosquitoes that had been the bane of Doc Coe's patients.

"Why did the city leaders allow this to happen right on Monument Circle?" I asked my father years later. During the 1970s, he explained, downtown was a workplace destination, nothing more.

So ever since its infancy, Indianapolis has managed to make it despite some ill-considered decisions. Not to mention an inaugural plague. Surely part of the way forward, now as then, is to listen to visionaries in our midst.

INDIANAPOLIS

KAITLYNNE MANTOOTH

Summer

Pool memories and
Hot pavement
And the flowers grow through the cracks next to
My neighbor who collects money on the street corner
He's a World War II veteran
Who likes friendship bracelets and
Knock Knock Jokes

The boys play basketball at the park
And the nights were lit by window panes
And fireflies who weren't afraid of the dark
And tall street lights who gave us advice
Likewise older brothers who wore colorful
Bandanas on their ankles

And we were not afraid
Of open doors and front porches
Because every front porch was a new
Kingdom
And the kings and queens shared
Their crockpot dinners
And backyard lemonade

And summer lasted forever back then
Under the shadow of Indianapolis skyscrapers
But we liked it best under the shadows
Because it was cooler

So we went fishing on the white river
Because that's where we kept our poles, in a nearby bush
And my toes still cry out for the cool water when I dream

And slowly the leaves change color

Fall

The sidewalks cool down
And are speckled with orange leaves
Like paint splashed on a cracked canvas
Uniformed boys and girls line up
On city corners
Waiting for sunset yellow buses to take them to school
And things are hopefully beginning to end
And things change and
My friend on the street corner
Puts on more layers and holds a sign that says
"Happy holidays and God Bless"

And kids prepare
And front porches prepare for Thanksgiving
And put up string lights

And then the first snow

Winter

The snow falls onto the abandoned houses
And covers the boarded windows
Like a wedding dress
And everything is more innocent
Because everything is inside

The night comes earlier
And we dress warmer and
Make snowmen out of dirty snow
And our neighbors invite us in for
Stories of family trees and hot chocolate
To stain our top lips

And my friend on the corner isn't on the corner
But under the underpass
Because he says it's warmer
But the salt trucks on 65 keep him up

And the string lights were bright
And merry christmas was on our lips
Even though times were tough
And santa might not be able to come
This year
But we sang the carols anyways

And then the new year and
We drank cheap wine and sang karaoke
Into the snowy night
And no one cared that it was cold
Or that the sidewalk was cracked and icy

And then the sun rises and the ice melts
And it is

Spring

And the morning glories make their way
up chain-link fences
And remind the city to wake up
So we drive to work on cracked roads
And spit curses at the potholes

But we are happy for the
50, 60, 70 degree weather
Even if it brings
Heavy rain and tornado warnings
Because we like to sit on the porch and watch the rain fall
And drink Folgers coffee

And the boys play basketball in torn-up shoes
On the weekends

But they have to be home in time to study
Because it's exam season
And the street lights still give advice to anyone who listens

And my friend on the corner
Holds a new sign
That just says "God Bless"
And he laughs at new jokes loudly
Because he's thankful for the flowers that grow in the cracks
So I make him a new friendship bracelet
Because that's what neighbors do

And the sun heats the pavement
Until it is

Summer

TIBBS DRIVE-IN

ANNE LAKER

Keep going past the puffy pecs of Mr. Bendo
the horse patrol by the old asylum
and the taco loco trucks
laced with light, smarting with cilantro.

Turn left at the hook-up hotel.
Get in line by the car part graveyard.

Pick your flick from among the four:
saucer-eyed cartoon cats or
ashen devil dolls or
brazen action jerks or
dudes in drag with padded asses.

The sun melts on the lilac horizon as fast as hot nitrate.
My malted milk melts too
paddled to the mouth with mini tongue depressor
while cicadas saw a soundtrack by the treeline.

Free yo-yo with purchase of sno-cone.

I love the vapists
and babies with orange soda in their bottles
and kids enthroned in lawn chairs in the beds of pick-ups.

My heart's gone with the prickled percussion of tires crushing gravel
and the dust, rising in the headlights, all roads
headed for holograms of Charlize Theron.

Bats star in the trailer advertising dusk

INDY 500, 1975

GRANT VECERA

A skeleton of a man, not too drunk,
in cutoffs and a patchy beard
clambered up from his lawn chair,
and flicked his cigarette
onto Mr. Nichols' perfect lawn
where we were playing it cool
on our Stingrays and skateboards—
except Mike, who could stay afloat
on his unicycle by rocking in place
as if it were as natural
as draining a cold one on a hot day.

"Ride that goddamn clown bike
down around them fellers on their motorsickles
and I'll give you this here five dollar bill!"
Blue smoke plumed
through his scabby nostrils
as the man said this.

Every spring our moms and dads said
to stay away from the sun burnt wahoos
idling tailgate to tailgate on Moller Road
with their precious, jostling ice chests
and magnificent stench of diesel, sweat,
and sweetly hissing charcoal.

HAWKING INDY 500 SOUVENIRS DURING THE 100TH RUNNING OF THE GREATEST SPECTACLE IN RACING

MICHAEL BROCKLEY

Aloha Shirt Man arranges merchandise in his booth. Tucked between a tent belonging to a preacher and a motorcycle mama kiosk carrying black velvet mementos. He fans autographed color glossies of Helio Castroneves and Danica Patrick across his card table. Hangs samples of t-shirts featuring Parnelli Jones and A. J. Foyt on a clothesline he has strung along the rear wall while Jim Nabors' greatest hits plays on his boombox. Nabors baritoning the moonlight on the Wabash. Aloha checks his cash box. Straightens the Ray Harroun biographies on his spinner rack. Fidgets with the rare Willy T. Ribbs hardback in its protective casing. The preacher in the next booth regales the first rush of customers, "I have fought the good fight, I have run the race." Aloha Shirt Man's first customer buys "A Month at the Brickyard" and a XXXL Mario Andretti t-shirt. As the traffic of race fans ebbs and flows, Aloha practices card tricks. Half-heartedly looks for the lost notes in a blues harmonica. In the Brickyard, the announcer broadcasts, "Ladies and gentlemen, start your engines," while Aloha thumbs through an outdated road atlas. As the Indy cars explode onto the straightaway, he gives the preacher his last Super Tex baseball cap with the scrambled eggs on the brim and leaves the black velvet merchant a Sarah Fisher t-shirt. He draws the awning down on his race day merchandise and charges into his future to find a wilderness prophet. To search for somewhere more welcoming than home.

THIS IS DOGTOWN

NASREEN KHAN

One day I bought a house on my lunch break.

It's a 1930's bungalow in "Clark's addition to Haughville" which is really just the Black part of Haughville before you get to what used to be the Slovenian part of Haughville, which is now the Mexican part of Haughville. It's not on the map like Stringtown or the bougie River West the new developers want to call it.

Walking home from the library last summer, pushing the stroller past the corner of Belmont and Michigan where a girl was killed in a drive-by one night after she got off her shift, there is a mural shrine to Courtney Paige who was a dancer at Patty's show club.

That summer my son was still in diapers the air hot as hell, and muggy like menudo on Sunday morning. He said *shh mama that dog is sleeping*, and stuck a chubby hand out the stroller shade and into the sun.

And it's true that dog was sleeping in the grass between the sidewalk and the road—right across from the pink and blue letters remembering Courtney Paige. Courtney Paige, born in the same year as me, on the same day as me. I don't know what day she died, so all I know is that her death shrine lists my birthday. I don't know what day she died, but I know her little girl, who's a little older than my son, likes to eat Kraft cheese singles between slices of wonder bread while she rides her bike down the sidewalk between her house and mine, and that when I moved here her aunt said *we've never had no trouble living here* and Courtney's little girl looked in my eyes and said *except for when my mama passed*.

And on the sidewalk across from Courtney Paige like he was laying at her feet—it's true that a dog was sleeping in the grass between the sidewalk and the road—a half-grown husky with its head on its paws sleeping with ants crawling out of empty eye sockets, half-covered in sweet fuzzy eyelashes, fat grubs falling out of his ears.

After I took my baby home for his nap and read him stories and kissed his brown cheeks and thought about getting a shovel myself, I called a whole bunch of numbers of places with names that seemed like they were supposed to help.

But there isn't an office, I guess, whose job it is to come and bury dead dogs on the Westside.

JIM JONES GOES TO NIGHT SCHOOL

NATE LOGAN

Looks like Elvis if he sold used cars.
"How can I demonstrate my Marxism?
The thought was, infiltrate the church."
A straight line from June 11–15, 1956
Cadle Tabernacle, to selling exotic pets,
to racial integration. A stick of dynamite
left in the Temple coal pile for his trouble.
In ten years, graduates from Butler (1961)
with a degree in secondary education.
Later, leaves Indiana. Does not end well.

PUNK ROCK IN NAPTOWN

STEPHANIE REID

Maybe the show will start at 10.
Hardcore!
Circle up!
All female band from Japan in an Eastside basement tonight.
Underground!
Circle up!
MDC at the Melody Inn.
Punk Rock Night at the Melody Inn.
Pit!
Circle up!
That chick can jam on those drums.
All ages welcome.
5 bucks to get in for 8 bands.
Circle up!
See you at the Emerson.
So hardcore in Fountain Square.
Circle up Naptown, circle up!

EAST SIDE

JACKIE LUTZKE

1.

At Kroger, after I've paid and am making my way toward the exit, past the carts of rejected merchandise, the freezer holding bags of ice, the claw game full of stuffed animals I won't let my son play because *it's a wasted quarter*, I see the Coinstar. There's a white sign stuck to the side: **Out of Order**. *It's always out of order*, I think, before I realize that a man is standing in front of the machine, successfully plunking change into the tray, the coins sliding away into the machine's belly.

Not presently out of order. But ready to be.

2.

I once overheard a man at a bar tell the bartender about his soon-to-be-ex (his words), how she's from Indonesia, how amazing the food is there. They were bonding over dishes, this man, this bartender, and that part is nice but the method was odd to me, invoking a broken or breaking relationship to facilitate a momentary here-and-now connection, or maybe it's just an act of sentiment, to draw forward facts in new contexts, another way to hold on, another way to say goodbye.

3.

10th Street between my house and downtown is obstructed for a segment by construction, and I forget this every time until I get to it. Then I change plan, change lane, turn right to head north, intending to dart westward at the next intersection. On the new route I passed a fenced-in lot with, for a segment, cloth of some kind wrapped around the rows of barbed wire at the top. This is unmissable in its starkness and its seeming lack of sense. I can't fathom why it's there.

I assume that whenever this happened it wasn't just moments ago, as one does—gives everything credit for an extensive backstory and uses that backstory to deepen or clarify bemusement.

4.

I went to a Redbox. Wondered if I shouldn't have because it was snowing and it's maybe supposed to be snowing tomorrow. Maybe that'd mean I couldn't return the movie on time. Then I thought, *heck, I can walk to the Redbox if needed. Heck, I can keep the movie TWO nights.*

I swiped my credit card. The screen to punch in my ZIP code popped up. I pressed 4… and froze. ZIP code: forgotten. Muscle memory: stalled out. And for a few seconds, before muscle memory kicked back on, I looked up at the falling snow and let myself be anywhere.

INDIANAPOLIS

FRAN QUINN

It is so cold today, no one runs past my house
to shave off a pound of last year's fat. They cherish
each ounce as coating for the aching bones.
It is late January whose two-faced god
looks to both the past and future. And it seems right
to me to worship anyone who gets me beyond
the misery of the present. Then a wisp of steam
comes out of my neighbor's dryer duct.

It rubs against my window like a ghost that wants in,
and I begin to pity steam and half-think I'll open up for him,
when the next ghost rises and, I swear, I see
a face I seem to know—and am startled
to recognize mad Willy Blake, Prince of the Eternal
Present, come to check out our chartered streets.
But no one in this city is mad enough to be out
on a day like this: "Only ghosts like you," I tell him.

"Maybe if you wander Indiana Ave. you can find
some of those brothers of Jazz or fathers of the Blues.
We destroyed their haunts. But they're still there,
just as in the old days, little praised and little honored,
but persistent. Or some gust will carry you
like Jesus to the top of the State House dome where D.C. Stephenson
might offer you his kingdom of the Klan for just a genuflection."
Then as if propelled by Blake's own voice, it is I
who am transported to the Wheeler Mission where men,
who look like ghosts, and women, barely alive, vie for a meal.
They were out all night. My heart sinks and I hear old mad Willy whisper
"marks of weakness, marks of woe," and I remember those jazzmen
hammering at the manacles our minds have forged, and those blues riffs
that formed, from the cold, their own long lines. But it was only
when Blake's ghost refused to enter my house, and took his place
among the poor, I saw on the window pane
a halo of ice around my breath as if the cold itself were the holy place.

IMAGINING THE BLACK CROSSROADS: MUSIC AND MEMORY ON INDIANA AVENUE

PAUL R. MULLINS AND JORDAN B. RYAN

Indiana Avenue is today mythologized as one of America's twentieth-century jazz hotbeds, its musical history revered by twenty-first-century Circle City boosters for whom jazz is an essential element of the city's cultural patrimony. Over more than a half-century planners and developers have imagined jazz as the heart of Avenue history. In 1982 the *Indianapolis News* sentimentally remembered Indiana Avenue jazz: "Not too long ago, Indianapolis had a flickering, beating heart.... Small clubs up and down Indiana Avenue jumped with jazz.... Zoot suits and slinky dresses. People laughing, clapping for what they'd come to hear. Jazz." Such fantasies of jazz and the Avenue routinely take pride in African American expressive culture, appropriate it as part of the city's shared heritage, and implicitly rationalize the urban renewal that razed the Indiana Avenue landscape. Nevertheless, developers, planners, and preservationists eager to celebrate Indiana Avenue's cultural heritage are left with little architecture to evoke its history, and the barren Avenue provides an unsettling testimony to urban renewal's devastation of Black life and community.

An *Indianapolis Star* columnist read the death rites to the Avenue in 1979 when he concluded that a visit to Indiana Avenue's "dilapidated buildings, vacant lots and burned-out houses is a sad journey into yesterday. Gone are the dazzling nightclubs and ballrooms that marked its heyday. Time finally has caught up with one of Indianapolis's oldest streets. Deterioration has threatened to make it just a memory." That apparently inevitable "deterioration" was the express intent of urban renewal projects that aspired to erase the African American Avenue even as the city lauded jazz memories. "Slum clearance," highway construction, and the establishment of Indiana University-Purdue University Indianapolis (IUPUI) gutted Indiana Avenue in the 1960s and 1970s, leaving most of the residential neighborhoods and Avenue clubs empty by 1980. Planners paint fanciful pictures of the Avenue, but empty lots and uninspired post-1970 architecture punctuate how racism shaped more than a century of African American expressive culture and marketing through segregation, displacement, and re-development.

Indiana Avenue continues to be fantasized by planners committed to the same re-development imagined by postwar urban renewal forces. The state, planners, ideologues, and developers extol a rather shallow notion of jazz heritage as a façade that incorporates historically African American places and their heritage without illuminating the persistence of structural racism. Since the 1960s, proposals to manufacture a newly profitable Avenue have lobbied for an accessible and appealing history that ignores how African Americans have been historically excluded from white public space and distorted in public memory.

Our interest is in the Avenue's heritage beyond a handful of postwar jazzmen, instead examining the breadth of expressive culture, commerce, and vice that intersected on the racially segregated Avenue. On the one hand, contemporary jazz celebrations avoid all the dimensions of Avenue life that unsettled white society and illuminated racial privilege; on the other hand, that everyday Avenue life including jazz was alluring to many whites eager to escape bourgeois behavioral codes. The urban renewal history of Indiana Avenue and its subsequent romanticization are common to many American cities leveled by postwar programs that disproportionately took aim at Black communities. Like many of those places, Indiana Avenue's heritage risks being distorted to accent contemporary gentrification fantasies and ignore the experience of anti-Black racism and structural inequality that Indiana Avenue's heritage narrates.

This photograph shows the 300-500 blocks of Indiana Avenue looking northwest near the intersection of Vermont Street, Senate Avenue, and Indiana Avenue, circa 1950s. The Walker Theatre can be seen in the background along Indiana Avenue. The Cotton Club Restaurant, seen on the right-hand side of the photograph, was located on the northeastern corner of Vermont Street and Senate Avenue at 242 West Vermont Street. A majority of buildings in this image have been demolished. *(Photo: City of Indianapolis, Department of Metropolitan Development, Indiana Historical Society)*

Imagining the Avenue

Indiana Avenue is one of four diagonal thoroughfares extending from Indianapolis's central circle as part of the 1821 "Mile Square" plan. A few African Americans were living in an integrated community along Indiana Avenue in the 1830s, and in the wake of the Civil War, almost 1000 African Americans were living on the Avenue and in the neighborhoods adjacent to the Avenue. The most profound social and demographic transformation of the Avenue came between 1900 and 1910 when two related historical processes changed Indianapolis and many more Northern cities. First, African Americans began arriving in Indianapolis as part of the "Great Migration." In 1900 15,931 Black people lived in Indianapolis, and a decade later that total had grown to 21,816 initiating a period of rapid African American population growth. Nearly all of these new residents were leaving the South to escape the emergence of legalized "Jim Crow" segregation and anti-Black violence. However, the second transformation that greeted them in the Circle City was racial segregation emerging locally at the turn of the twentieth century. Newcomers to the Circle City would not experience the legal segregation they left in the South, but *de facto* segregation of public spaces, residential settlement, and eventually schools would strictly govern everyday public rights and create a segregated predominately African American neighborhood along Indiana Avenue.

Music and theater were always the heart of African American life, with performances in churches, schools, public halls, and private homes. African Americans appeared in some predominately white theaters downtown, and a handful of Avenue clubs and theaters began to feature African American performers in the late-nineteenth and early twentieth-century. However, there were not enough performance spaces for an African American performer to do more than earn a modest supplementary income. Consequently, Indianapolis's most talented turn-of-the-century African American performers joined tent troupes that traveled throughout the country performing for white audiences as well as African Americans. Into the 1940s such traveling troupes performed theater shows whose song, dance, and minstrelsy invoked racist caricatures of Southern Black captivity even as they placed African American expressive culture at the heart of American popular culture. For instance, Salem Tutt Whitney and his brother Homer Tutt were among Indianapolis's earliest generation of African American traveling performers. Salem Tutt was born in Logansport, Indiana in about 1876, attended Indianapolis's Shortridge High School, and was living in Indianapolis in 1894 when he first toured with a traveling troupe known as the Tennessee Warblers. His brother Homer joined him as they performed music, theater, and dance with a series of well-known national companies leading up to Sherman Houston Dudley's Smart Set company, performing in vaudeville and eventually motion pictures into the 1930s.

Around 1910 a series of theaters opened along the Avenue offering up vaudeville, music, and cinema for the growing African American neighborhood. The Two Johns Theater, for instance, was a white-owned stage and cinema that opened in the 700 block of Indiana Avenue in 1908. John B. Hubert and John A. Victor's theater had an orchestra pit and stage for musical and vaudeville performances presented alongside silent films, and the Two Johns remained open as a cinema until 1959. The Crown Garden opened in 1910 as an open-air stage on Indiana Avenue lots that backed onto the Central Canal, and in July 1910 an ad in the *Indianapolis Recorder* touted the Crown Garden as "the best Colored theatre between New York and Chicago." However, in September 1910 the neighboring Columbia Theatre advertised itself as the "only first class theatre owned and operated solely by colored people in this city," a thinly veiled reference to the Crown's ownership by a white feed store merchant, Roland Geyer.

These early theaters were distinguished by a performance tradition in which nearly any form of music, comedy, dance, and drag would appear on the stage any given night. In 1911, for instance, Tim Owsley took over management of the Crown Garden. Owsley was a veteran African American songwriter and performer who had traveled throughout the country since about 1901, and he purchased the theater in 1912 and was screening silent movies alongside theatrical performances and music. Nearly all of the Avenue's earliest theaters were showing silent movies on the eve of World War I alongside theater and music. For example, the Pioneer Theatre opened at 515 Indiana Avenue in November 1913, and while it would primarily screen silent films, its opening night performance featured a stage show by Indianapolis performer Frank Fowler Brown. The Pioneer's opening night featured one of the very earliest African American motion pictures, *The Butler*, a movie produced by the Foster Photoplay Company. *The Butler*'s star, Lottie Grady, was a well-known vaudeville performer who appeared at the Crown Garden in 1912 and 1915. Indianapolis excursions were held expressly to go to Chicago and see "Colored Pictures" that included films by the Foster Photoplay Company, which formed in 1910. But few communities had a sufficiently large population to support segregated African American movie houses or film companies, and African American moviemakers like Foster were unable to reach significant audiences beyond densely settled African American urban communities; Foster's company folded in 1917.

No space on the Avenue was more famed than the Walker Theatre, which opened in 1927 and had a theater, ballroom, businesses, and professionals' offices alongside the Walker Company's offices. The building was dedicated to Madam C. J. Walker, the cosmetics entrepreneur who died in 1919. The Walker's opening program on December 26, 1927 featured Reginald DuValle's "Blackbirds" orchestra alongside a showing of the silent film "The Magic Flame." Born in 1893, DuValle was among the nation's earliest jazz performers, with his professional career starting in ragtime before 1910. DuValle would have a long career playing alongside all of Indianapolis's most prominent African American ragtime and jazz performers as well as many white musicians including Hoagy Carmichael.

The DuValle orchestra including Reginald's older brother Sylvester was performing throughout central Indiana from about 1912, and under Reginald's direction, they were being referred to as "DuVall's [sic] Jazz Orchestra" by 1917. In July 1915 Gordon Seagrove was the first documented observer to use the term "jazz" to describe "harmonious, yet discordant wailing" that he suggested "started in the south half a century ago and are the interpolations of darkies originally. The trade name for them is 'jazz.'" In October 1917, Earle J. Marsh's dance studio at North and Illinois Streets began to feature music by DuValle's orchestra, which became one of the city's first jazz bands when it was billed as "DuValle's Cabaret and Jazz Orchestra," "DuValle's Syncopated Jazz Orchestra," or "DuValle's Camouflage Orchestra." DuValle's band played performances for the white dance studio with a band billed as a "company of live wires! You just can't make your feet behave when they play those irresistible tunes." Performers like DuValle would play the Avenue clubs, but much of their livelihood came from playing for white audiences at regional events and in venues like the Marsh dance studio.

Much of the commerce on Indiana Avenue existed at the borders of the law since the late nineteenth century. For instance, one of the Avenue's earliest African American entrepreneurs, Archie Greathouse, was born into slavery in 1858 and became a Pullman porter when his family came to Indianapolis after the Civil War. Greathouse applied for his first Avenue liquor permit in 1889 and over four decades his saloons became gathering places for gambling that were subject to recurring raids. In 1903 the *Indianapolis Journal* suggested that "Among the places that gave Indiana avenue a bad name, none has been more notorious than that of Archie Greathouse." Yet Greathouse was considered a generous philanthropist and grassroots activist among many of the Avenue's audiences. For instance, Greathouse had never attended school himself, but he funded lawyers in the 1920s to appeal the Ku Klux Klan-supported School Board's plans for the complete segregation of city schools. In 1923 he filed a suit seeking the right for his daughter to attend Indianapolis Public School 36 in his neighborhood at 28th and Capitol, and a year later he was the plaintiff in a case seeking to stop the construction of a separate Black high school. In March 1926 the State Supreme Court finally rejected Greathouse's case, which allowed construction to continue on Crispus Attucks High School.

In the 1920s there was clearly a furtive white fascination with African American expressive culture, and moralists and city officials began to patrol forays by whites onto the Avenue. For example, Archie Young transformed his saloon into a soda parlor when Prohibition began, and he orchestrated dice games that led the *Indianapolis Times* to call it a "notorious gambling place." Young's establishment at 532 ½ Indiana Avenue became known as the Golden West Cabaret, and during a December 1921 raid a series of white customers "were found in the place listening to the jazz orchestra that plays the syncopated music, as it is only found on 'de Avenoo.'" Archie Young argued there was no law preventing whites from frequenting an African American venue, and the police responded that "they are aware there is no law to prevent white persons from visiting the cabarets, but they contend they can take names and search those who are found there." The police provided the names of four of the white customers to the newspaper as a deterrent and emphasized that they would keep raiding the club "until the white persons are eliminated." Two days later the *Star* reported that "last night white folk, attracted down the avenue in hope of spending an hour or two in Young's establishment, reputed to be so delightfully wicked, were politely shooed away."

Young was a Republican party fixture nicknamed "Joker," and his cabaret routinely had a jazz orchestra performing. The *Indianapolis Star* suggested that "White persons visiting the place in recent weeks, ostensibly to hear a special brand of syncopated dark town music and enjoy the invigorating fizz from Joker's elaborate and shiny soda fountain, have in reality been attracted because the place is one of the few cabarets, black or white, in town that is open after midnight." Yet the newspaper conceded the fascination of Avenue nightlife and African American expressive culture, acknowledging that "it got to be quite the thing for venturesome young men to take their sweethearts and young wives to the place for an hour or two of shivery entertainment, the innocents shivering to think how degrading and bohemian it was for whites to mix carelessly with the negroes sitting at adjoining tables, listening to the same music watching the dancing and replenishing glasses surreptitiously from concealed bottles." The venue was rumored to condone racially mixed dance, and the *Star* indicated that "reports were current that White girls frequenting the place danced with colored bucks and vice versa. The proprietor, however, insists it has always been his policy to preserve racial lines." In February 1924 the police once again raided the Golden West and charged Young with a violation of liquor laws, and the cabaret closed when Young and Harry "Goosie" Lee were sentenced to six months at the Indiana State Farm. Young and Lee resumed control of the Golden West after their release, re-naming it the Hollywood. Lee would manage a series of clubs in the 500 block until his death in 1943.

Few of the Avenue's entrepreneurs were more prominent than brothers Denver and Sea Ferguson. Denver Ferguson came to Indianapolis in 1919, and the printer produced lottery slips that became part of a gambling operation managed with his brother. In 1927 Denver filed articles of incorporation opening a restaurant, the Rainbow Palm Garden, and Sea opened the Trianon Ballroom in December 1931. At the end of Prohibition, Sea opened the Cotton Club in 1933 in the building that held his Trianon Ballroom and Denver opened one of the Avenue's most famous clubs, the Sunset Terrace, in December 1937. The Fergusons were among the most influential club owners in the "Chitlin' Circuit," a network of Southern and Midwestern clubs and theaters in which African Americans performed beginning around 1940.

The Ferguson clubs hosted many of the nation's most prominent musicians, and many of these acts attracted white fans. However, twenty-first-century fantasies of jazz uniting white and Black fans in Avenue clubs ignores that ideologues on both sides of the color line were wary of interracial leisure. On March 18, 1939, an African American on neighboring California Street, Emma Lewis, wrote the *Indianapolis Recorder* and complained that African Americans were "making complaints against the Sunset Terrace, owned and operated by a colored citizen, because he catered to white patrons as well as colored. While they are trying to bar the white patrons away from the Terrace, they are also running Mr. Ferguson out of business because there are not enough colored people that have the money to spend to keep the Sunset Terrace in business." Lewis indicated that she and her husband David "go there once or twice a month" but believed that "there are not enough patrons to keep open." Lewis indicated she and her husband had been to a show at the Sunset on March 11, when the Whitman Sisters opened an engagement. The Whitman Sisters were a well-known African American vaudeville act that had toured since 1900, but Lewis indicated that "there was only 30 or 40 colored patrons there. There were about 250 white patrons turned away because of the complaints of their patronage." A week after Lewis's letter, Indianapolis Police conducted a raid on the Sunset Terrace and Cotton Club to "prevent social intermingling of races in night revelry." Police Chief Michael Morrissey acknowledged that he had "warned the operators previously that white persons must not be permitted to patronize establishments catering particularly to colored persons. But the warnings obviously were ignored." In April the *Recorder* reported that Chief Morrissey confirmed that "White people were ordered barred from Indiana avenue taverns." Morrissey may have verified

Emma Lewis's account when he told the *Recorder* the raids were a response to "complaints of law violation" from "substantial citizens."

Some of these African American venues were managed by white entrepreneurs. One of the best-known clubs emerging in the wake of Prohibition was the Mitchellyn, which opened at 408-410 Indiana Avenue in August 1933. Joe Mitchell migrated to Indianapolis from Russia in January 1922, changing his name from Josef Mutchnik and coming to Indianapolis because his brother-in-law Sam Zukerman was managing a soda parlor on Massachusetts Avenue. In August 1923 Mitchell's parents and three siblings followed him to Indianapolis, including Joe's youngest brother Srul Mutchnik, who came to be known as Isaac "Tuffy" Mitchell. Joe Mitchell began managing a billiards hall and restaurant on the Avenue in 1923, and when Prohibition ended it became a restaurant and nightclub. Mitchell's billiard hall was from the outset a center for gambling and illegal alcohol sales. In June 1925, for instance, 36 men were arrested at the pool hall for gambling—"some colored and some white"—and consuming alcohol from Mitchell's "blind tiger." Sporadic arrests continued at Mitchell's billiards hall through the remainder of Prohibition for alcohol sales and gambling alike.

Joe Mitchell's younger brother Tuffy became part of the operation in the early 1930s, and Tuffy managed an ambitious gambling operation from the Mitchellyn and series of other family-controlled venues on and beyond the Avenue. In early 1940 Joe Mitchell went before the State Alcohol Beverage Commission facing a threat to revoke his liquor license following a murder at the saloon. The *Indianapolis Star* was a persistent critic of Mitchell and Avenue vice, and its editors celebrated that almost a hundred people attended the hearing, "most of them Negroes who have demanded that the license not be renewed." A host of African Americans were indeed committed to eradicating vice on the Avenue, and the *Indianapolis Recorder* joined the chorus of critics eager to close Mitchell's bar. Mitchell abandoned his application for a liquor license, but the pool room remained open and continued to be raided repeatedly for gambling.

Mitchell and his brother Tuffy surreptitiously controlled a series of clubs and liquor licenses in venues managed by a web of family members and allies. Tuffy by one count was arrested 34 times by 1951, and in 1952 he was arrested for a gambling operation that was centered in his café at 448 Indiana Avenue. Joe opened a liquor store on Indiana Avenue that he eventually turned over to his son Morris in 1954, just before Joe's death in March 1955. Morris began to work as a bail bondsman with an Indiana Avenue office in the late 1950s, and in 1966 he opened the Frederick Douglass Social Club at 421 Indiana Avenue. The club hosted music and dance shows alongside gambling until an October 1968 vice raid arrested 284 people at the club. Into the 1970s Morris Mitchell managed restaurants throughout Indianapolis and had connections to national organized crime as well as the Indianapolis Police Department and Marion County Republican Party.

When the Blue Eagle Inn opened in October 1933, the *Indianapolis Recorder* acknowledged that in the immediate wake of Prohibition the club expected "to do a thriving wine, whisky and song business." The inn was owned and managed by Joe Sarbinoff, a Macedonian immigrant who migrated to the United States in 1914 and managed an Indianapolis billiards hall and restaurant on Washington Street in the mid-1920s, where he was twice arrested for liquor law violations. The Blue Eagle sat at the corner of Indiana Avenue and California Street, and like many Avenue spaces the Blue Eagle was equal measures restaurant and nightclub offering up "sandwiches, chili, and chop suey" and a "special Bulgarian hot stew" with live and recorded music over nearly four decades. The club eventually moved across California Street to 701 Indiana Avenue in 1960, where the new space featured exotic dancers. The club remained there until 1970 (after which it first became the New Yorker Lounge, then Billy Mac's Lounge in October 1971, and finally Club 701 in November 1975).

The stereotype of the lone jazz guitarist in a smoke-filled postwar Avenue club ignores that some African American vaudeville traditions flourished in Avenue venues beyond World War II. For instance, William and Margie Benbow opened the Stormy Weather Café in about 1943 at 319 Indiana Avenue. In 1897 William Benbow joined the Old Virginia Cheroots tobacco company show performing the cakewalk, an improvisational dance that became popular in the 1870s and was a staple of early early-twentieth-century vaudeville. After serving in the Spanish-American War, Benbow managed a series of vaudeville troupes that toured the United States and then Cuba, Jamaica, and Panama.

William Benbow managed a series of Indianapolis clubs in the 1940s, and Benbow's spectacular shows borrowed from the burlesque, drag, and racy comedy that had been at the heart of African American vaudeville. In May 1941 the *Recorder* reported that "Wm. Benbow, producer of the red hot floor shows at the swank Supper Club, located on the second floor of the Cotton Club, Vermont and Senate, promises a brand new show with plenty of hotchu and pretty girls for Sunday night…. If you enjoy 'Flesh' shows, come out and give this rendezvous of merriment a play." The Log Cabin Club opened its doors at 524 Indiana Avenue in 1939, and under Benbow's management in April 1944 the Log Cabin was "currently presenting a sparkling floor show, [with] such outstanding performers as Bobby Lanay, strip tease dancer." A month later Benbow's show featured "Barbara Tania, queen of the strip teasers; Ophelia Hoy, blues singer; Laura Roney, chirper of sweet songs and local favorite: Ivy Anderson, female impersonator; Doris Duchess White, emcee and torch singer plus Fred Wisdom's orchestra."

Doris "Duchess" White appeared in many regional clubs beginning as early as March 1936, when White played Columbus, Ohio's Turf Club following "a tour of the eastern and western states" that would include 1936 shows in Chicago and 1937 performances in Cincinnati. In October 1940 the *Recorder* reported on White's shows in Nashville and observed that "she is quite a favorite with the act and is also noted as a musician and has played with a few name bands. The 'Duchess' sends greetings to many relatives and friends in Naptown and especially her co-work-ers [sic] at the Cotton Club. In private life the 'Duchess' is known as George Edward Hall, and lives at 923 E. 16th street, Indianapolis."

Female impersonators were a staple of vaudeville performance across the color line since the 19th century, and some of those performances unsettled moral ideologues. In July 1933, for instance, the *Recorder*'s Charlie Davis told his readers that "If you want to have the time of your life, don't fail to see the Pansie Floor Show at the Paradise Gardens next Thursday." Yet a week later the *Recorder* editorialists were outraged that "Indianapolis has had its first 'fairy' (fag) (pansy) public stage show and dance. Fifteen young men (actually a misnoner) [sic] changed the conventional garb of their sex last Thursday night, bedecked themselves in female attire that shriveled the heart of many a true member of the weaker sex with envy, and proceeded to give a first class 'girl' show to the utter delight of 2000 thrill seekers." The *Recorder* called the show "a disgrace to this community.... The surprisingly heavy patronage netted by the contemptible program from supposedly self-respecting men and women in all walks of life in this community is condemnable in the strongest of terms." The *Recorder* urged the police to prevent drag shows, calling the performers and audiences "a pitiable group of allegedly confirmed degenerates."

This photograph shows the intersection of Ohio Street and Illinois Street facing northwest along Indiana Avenue, circa 1970s. This is the first block of Indiana Avenue before it became vacated in order to make way for the AUL Insurance Tower (now One America Tower). An auto service center and loan service company building are featured across from each other at the former terminus of Indiana Avenue. *(Photo: City of Indianapolis, Department of Metropolitan Development, Indiana Historical Society)*

Imagining Blight

The processes that emptied Indiana Avenue in the 1960s are much like the urban renewal projects that took aim on nearly all American cities. Slum caricatures had targeted historically African American neighborhoods since the early twentieth century, and such rhetoric intensified after World War II. In 1953 the *Indianapolis Star* ran a series on the impact of slum life and indicated that the "disease and rat-infested sties and rookeries are more vile than even our reproduced photographs will reveal…. Some scenes from the slums are so revolting as to offend even the most hardened viewer." This rhetoric championed wholesale eradication of "blighted" neighborhoods and imagined the historically African American near-Westside would become a blank canvas for planners to re-develop.

That development happened in the form of state programs committed to "slum clearance" projects, and their impact was magnified by highway construction that leveled even more African American neighborhoods while Indiana University built an undergraduate campus and expanded the Medical Center in the 1960s and 1970s. Between 1945 and 1962 the Indianapolis Redevelopment Commission conducted 12 "slum clearance" projects razing 576 total acres. In 1958 the Commission produced a master design for the city's downtown that aspired to erase "blighted areas," on the one hand, that targeted transformations in the neighborhoods along Indiana Avenue, but, on the other hand, the Commission design planned to leave the area a residential neighborhood and create green spaces along the White River. The design proposed to develop a joint undergraduate campus for Indiana and Purdue Universities alongside the Indiana University Medical Center, where medical students had been trained since the turn of the century. Planners advocated creating housing for Medical and Dental School students by clearing some predominately African American neighborhoods, but it only envisioned two blocks for the undergraduate campus.

That university would eventually be called Indiana University-Purdue University Indianapolis (IUPUI), and property for the campus began to be purchased by Indiana University starting in about 1964. By the time ground was broken for the first three IUPUI academic buildings in September 1968, the University had gone well beyond the 1958 master plan, acquiring over 2000 individual house lots as well as a handful of churches and businesses. The University acquired only a modest slice of property along the Avenue, but the campus's growth rapidly de-populated the neighborhoods whose residents had frequented Avenue venues for most of a half-century.

The University's expansion came at nearly the same moment that the state was clearing much of African American Indianapolis for interstates. In 1957 the state announced the plan to build Interstate 65 through Indianapolis as part of a route from Chicago to Louisville. The provisional plan for the route for I-65 through the near-Northside was proposed by engineers in January 1960, surveying had begun by 1961, and by November 1963 property acquisition began in Indianapolis. In May 1961 the *Indianapolis Recorder* concluded in despair that "the battle is lost. Many Northside residents who, earlier last year, tried in vain to get Interstate 65 built anywhere except on the route proposed by the State Highway Department, are chiefly concerned now with the relocation and depreciation value of their homes." Grassroots activists argued that the University and highway planners shared a common ambition to displace the African American community along Indiana Avenue. In October 1966, for instance, the community advocates

Homes Before Highways accused "the highway department and the university of browbeating homeowners in the path of the... inter-state highway system and the Westside residents whose homes occupy land wanted by the school for the expansion of its Indianapolis campus." Homes Before Highways charged "that Negroes are also being coerced, especially by representatives of Indiana University, to sell their homes at prices far below what it would take to find similar dwellings at today's prices."

This photograph shows the intersection of Indiana Avenue, West Street, and Michigan Street in the 1980s. Prominent buildings include the Walker Theatre, Lockefield Gardens, and the Miller Center. Most of the area shown is part of the Ransom Place neighborhood and the near westside neighborhood prior to IUPUI acquisition and expansion. *(Photo: Banayote Photo Inc., Indiana Historical Society)*

Urban Planning and Jazz Heritage

In 1968 a group of African Americans and city planners convened hoping to rescue Indiana Avenue in a project they dubbed "Operation Avenue." Like nearly all of the neighborhood development projects to follow, the project focused its re-development plan on the ways jazz history might influence future commerce and leisure. The *Indianapolis Star* reported that "one idea for the area which had been proposed would have created a 'Bourbon Street' atmosphere on the avenue. Bourbon Street is an entertainment section in New Orleans known as the birthplace of jazz music."

Operation Avenue's 1968 proposal to transform the Avenue into an urban retail and leisure district celebrating its African American musical heritage has been repeated continually over the subsequent half-century. The Avenue's reputation for being a hotbed of African American music is well-deserved, and ragtime, blues, jazz, gospel, and swing were part of a performance landscape that included cakewalks, vaudeville, minstrelsy, Shakespearean theatre, dance, burlesque, drag, and cinema. Nevertheless, ideologues have routinely ignored the breadth of African American expressive culture and a rich commercial leisure landscape. The longstanding enchantment with jazz and African American expressive culture betrays a furtive white fantasy of Blackness. Jazz looms in white imagination as an unfeigned expression of desire and resistance to bourgeois discipline, much as minstrel shows and vaudeville racism allowed white audiences to entertain their covert fascination with Blackness. These dominant histories concede segregation but largely ignore the ways racism rationalized the de-population of the Avenue and African American neighborhoods through-out the postwar United States. In the dominant twenty-first-century jazz fantasy, segregation appears as a sad history with an ironically rich artistic response that can now be consumed by appreciative audiences in an apparently "post-racial" moment.

RED CLAY

CHRIS SPECKMAN

if art is a lubricant for economic development,
what happens when it's not applied generously

to both partners as directed—the city & its residents?
no one pays respect to the mural of mari evans

on the broadside of a dog bakery, even though
she would have turned 100 today unbeknownst

to any soul whose name isn't graffiti
on the ungentrified walls of the chatterbox,

where light & dark liquor sits on the same stoop,
a desegregated neighborhood. proximity is everything.

you might mistake the three-story poet for the world's greatest
parking lot attendant with her ability to keep a straight face

as the monthly rate shoots up in the shadows
like the junkies conjured to justify white flight.

of all this area's hip ephemera, I am most transfixed
by the frohawked teen traversing the fragmented

curb stop as if it were a tightrope strung across the skyline.
he's the only one waiting for the bus, born under

a zoning covenant that won't go away like the second-
guessed signature blended in red clay beneath the crook

of mari's pink cardigan: *ALKEMI*. the texture, an echo.
what freddie hubbard transliterated for trumpet

upon witnessing a woman crammed in a trashcan,
the melody recycled by my favorite tribe

track about the seductiveness of the n-word & who can
get fucked. this is the cost of progress, everything lost

on followers whose hearts are artless, planned
avenues sans malice where art is heartless.

LEAVING INDIANA AFTER X-MAS, 1987

ETHERIDGE KNIGHT

I hitch a ride to the Air/Port
With a dude named "Red"
Who works as a Sky/Cap
In the Air/Port, who is a man,
And a proper/person. Red said:

"In my book, money talks, / (including tips),
And bullshit walks, and bullshit
Is alright, in fact, with bullshit I find no fault—
It's just that money talks, in *my* book."

I never see my children, I complain,
And count the coins in my jeans.
My mother is old and arthritic, I complain,
And I count the few coins in my jeans.
Fortune does not favor me, I sing
Is fewness forever my fare.

Leaving Indiana after X-mas, 1987

I hitch a ride to the AirPort,
With a dude named "Red"
Who works as a Sky/Cap
In the AirPort, who is a man,
And a proper/person. Red said:

"In my book, money talks/(including tips).
And bullshit walks, and bullshit
is alright, in fact with bullshit I find no fault_
It's just that money talks, in my book.

I never see my children, I complain,
And count the coins in my jeans
My mother is old and arthritic, I complain,
And I count the few coins in my jeans
Fortune does not favor me, I sing,
do fairness forgive my fare,

"Leaving Indiana after X-Mas, 1987" by Etheridge Knight, facsimile *(courtesy of Elizabeth McKim)*.

BUSKING ON
STATE CAPITAL STREETS

NORBERT KRAPF

The homeless drift on capital streets
in a city that should have been
named Tecumseh, Indiana.

Politicians fill the statehouse
copper dome with stale hot air.

Jazz solos lift toward
a full moon, circle around it,
and drop into Lucas Oil Stadium.

Wes Montgomery and Etheridge Knight
busk as a duo on Indiana Avenue.

WHAT WAS THE CONTRIBUTION OF NEIGHBORS?

TERRANCE HAYES

In 2005, I interviewed [Etheridge] Knight's sister Eunice Knight-Bowens during my visit to Indianapolis to read in her 14th Annual Etheridge Knight Festival. The reading took place in a suburban mall in Indianapolis. Eunice had inaugurated the festival in 1992, a year after her brother's death from cancer. The roster included local poets who knew Knight, local high school students who might be the next Etheridge Knight, and poets like me who were drawn by Knight's ghost: Sonia Sanchez, his ex-wife; Amiri Baraka, his peer; groups of brother poets like John Murillo and Reginald Dwayne Betts. After a twenty-year run the festival ended in 2012, a year before Eunice passed away. What was the contribution of neighbors? The festival was made of, by, and for the neighbors of Indianapolis. Etheridge's Indianapolis, Eunice's Indianapolis: When Eunice looked into the window of her brother's poetry she saw her own stories reflected. Did she know from the get-go that her brother was a great, rare kind of poet? I can't say. I know she was happy that I came asking for stories. She put me up in a hotel Knight used to frequent. She said all the Black writers met there to talk art and literature, but I was imagining all the booze, tobacco, and jive. The hotel room smelled of the cabbage she brought me and the cigarettes we smoked. I pushed the button on a small tape recorder. "I want people just to tell their stories about Knight, and everything is to come out of those stories," I told Eunice. She didn't miss a beat:

"A lot of his poems, like 'The Idea of Ancestry,' were written while he was in prison, in 'the belly of the beast' as he called it," she said almost automatically. I now know she'd told the story behind the poem many times. So had her brother. "He memorized it, he said, to save his sanity. The aunts were true, the cousins. It's just a true poem."

Some of what she said contradicted what I'd read about Knight's incarceration, some of what she said complicated what I'd read about his life. Knight may well be chief contributor to the lopsided details surrounding his life before imprisonment. Around whatever was his essential, inexplicable self were several identities: southerner, Black, son, male, convict, poet. Around those identities were also several biographical holes, gaps, and mysteries. He was the third of seven children and third son of Etheridge Sr. and Belzora Cozart-Knight. I did not ask Eunice why he, and not one of his older brothers, Charles and Floydell, was named after his father. Regrettably, I did not interview any of his other living siblings. His mother and father were dead by then, his brother Charles and sister Lois were dead by then. I sat in one chair and Eunice sat in the other. She wore a blue headscarf and a skin the shade of her brother's skin. She and her brother, she said, came from a long line of storytellers.

"My mother said that when they were little, before they went out to do their chores and before they went to school every morning, her oldest brother, my uncle Cid, played the organ and they had to sing. And so my mother could sing 'do re mi' without music, and so every morning before they went out to do their chores and before they went to school, they had to sing music as an art."

A sharp biographer will definitely need to find all of Knight's surviving relatives, his lovers and ex-lovers, his students, his son, Isaac BuShie Blackburn-Knight. I interviewed Mary Karr, who was one of Knight's students. I've interviewed his editor, Ed Ochester. I've interviewed and gossiped with or made plans to interview and gossip with maybe half a dozen other friends of Knight over the years. I've come nowhere close to gathering enough "facts" for a biography. I have not examined Knight's prison or war records; I have not interviewed inmates or staff at the jails and prisons; I have not interviewed the students of the Free People's Workshop. What was the contribution of neighbors? I have not interviewed his teammates on the army football team in Korea, the soldiers within earshot of his jive and tirades, the nurses who nursed him in rehab, the junkies or pushers who knew him. I have not interviewed Knight's lovers: Sonia Sanchez, Mary McAnally, Evelyn Brown, Elizabeth McKim, Charlene Blackburn. Knight's future biographer will have a lengthy chapter on romance. If we are lucky, someday some future biographer will land in Indianapolis and rent a small car and buy a map on his way to the Indiana State Prison or the factory where Knight worked as a punch-press operator during the five months of his parole or to 555 Massachusetts Avenue where Knight died in 1991 of lung cancer. If the future biographer's book is made into a movie, one hopes tropes of the blues and bluesman don't simplify Knight's life. It's an unreasonable hope, maybe. A life has to be simplified if it is to have shape, arc, trajectory: a biography needs a plot. Knight's story doesn't require much, I suppose. A couple of visits to Corinth, Mississippi, where he was born. To Paducah, Kentucky. I once thought a life was simply the accumulation of ideas, but now I think it may simply be the accumulation of details. Somewhere between detail and idea is the truth. Knight was often blowing smoke, as they say. And to write a biography one would need to gather all that smoke into something solid, something you could hold and turn over in your hands. "The Idea of Ancestry" almost suggests the *idea* of a biography is better than an actual biography.

Excerpt from To Float in the Space Between: A Life and Work in Conversation with the Life and Work of Etheridge Knight *(Wave Books, 2018). —Ed.*

MY FATHER'S KEEPER

ASHLEY MACK-JACKSON

After Etheridge Knight and for my father

1

There are no pictures of my father
up in our house. We only say his name after
9. After dinner when we are all huddled
together in my mother's bed and the cordless
phone passes between our stiff fingers. We say *Hi
Daddy* slow like the words sting our mouths.
My mother just says *your father, your father*
and places the cold plastic in our hands, one
after the other. Oldest, me, then the baby.
This is the only quiet hour of the day in our

house. The rest is running water, pounding feet
and Boys II Men and Duck Tales and Mortal
Kombat and *shut up* and *leave me alone.* (Nobody
asks about daddy). We are happy (except Mommy
who closes the door behind her and does not say
a word). No one cries.

My sister is Aarika (with double A's like my father
Aaron). My name is Ashley (after my great-grand
father). My brother is Aaron Joshua (we always say
both names so no one gets confused). The A is the only
thing that reminds me of Daddy. In first period when I write
my name on the top of a paper, before the subject,
before the date I think about the day we went to the City
Market and had shrimp fried-rice on the patio. Then I think
about my dead grandpa. Mommy gave me a picture of him
standing next to a rusty red and white Mustang holding a beer
in one hand and a wrench in the other (I think I must be more like him.)

2

The road trip is just like going to Kings Island. Grandma fries
chicken and waits on the porch swing with a foil wrapped Pyrex
dish resting on her lap. We pack a cooler and tapes (gospel and Marvin
Gaye because Grandma's ears can't take rap). The city street turns into a four
lane highway with cars whipping past us and blue rest stop signs. When we
are hungry, and ask for McDonald's, Grandma passes us chicken wings
wrapped in flowery napkins, and we forget the golden arches
and Ronald. Mommy says that we are still in Indiana but I don't believe
it could be the same place with the houses set so far back from the street
that they don't look real. We play eye spy and Outburst Travel until the one lane
is lined with red dust that kicks up around our Caravan windows,
and we remember where the road leads. We remember the gray
penitentiary walls. In that last thirty minutes everything is still.
Everything is quiet except the occasional crackle of the tiny rocks that
pop against the belly of the van.

Now Daddy is on the other side of a round table. There is not
enough space between us to pretend he isn't here, and I concentrate
on the other people in the room. There is a woman with a blond
boy curled up in her lap. They are both sobbing. I look at my brother
and sister. No one cries for Daddy.

IN INDY, #BLACKYOUTHMATTER!

DAROLYN "LYN" JONES

For me, the beauty and power of this city are the voices that lie beyond the margins, the voices at the fringe. Superhero children without capes or an S on their chest, who instead yield their power and their resistance through words.

Through the Indiana Writers Center's Public Memoir Project, I've been teaching creative narrative nonfiction writing to 250 plus students in the underserved neighborhoods of Indianapolis since 2010. The day after the Zimmerman/Martin trial came down in 2014, driving down Central to our largest site, the Saint Florian Center for Youth Leadership and Development, run by the Black Firefighter's Union, I came upon protestors in these streets.

I entered the former IPS School #27 in the Kennedy-King neighborhood, one that rarely makes the maps or books. The air can't keep up in the old building, and we often have to step over unwelcome guests, rats from older vacant houses or dying trees in the nearby park, and roaches—all in search of the snack food that often falls on the floor from young hands. Four years of working eight weeks with the same students. Four years of young Black, future leaders trusting me with their stories. It all stopped that day. Entering—no high five's, no hugs, no hellos. The writers were quiet, sober, looking at me with distrust, confusion, even contempt.

Was I still an ally, an advocate for them? Or was I a white face that might exploit or hurt them?

I sat down and joined the quiet. I looked up at them with as much intent, integrity, and trust as a face could conjure at that moment, difficult when my own heartache and anger at the power one man in another part of the country could have on *my* kids and in *my* city.

"Tell me what it's like to be a young and Black living in this city. Tell me about a time when someone told you or made you to feel like your Black life didn't matter."

They sat there, uneasy, unsure how to proceed. They looked towards their unspoken, leader. He stood up, visibly angry, and said with a calm and suddenly adult, stern voice, "You have no idea how hard it is."

"You're right. I don't. But you know what I do know? That writing is a way to resist, to protest, to tell the world what it's really like. You are the only ones who can. Because you do know."

A seven-year-old wrote about a woman who yanked her backpack pulling her behind everyone in line because Black girls go last, a high school student talked about the last few minutes of football championship facing off with a white opponent he had played with and known for eight years. The ball was snapped, and his friend, called him a "no good, N—". A ten-year old writes about switching schools and being made fun of because of her hair and dress. But when she straightened her hair and changed the way she dressed, everyone, even the teacher, was suddenly nicer to her. And then there were stories about uncles, cousins, friends, even fathers who had been treated unfairly and violently by the local police and the judicial system.

Since 2014, too many more names have been added to the list below Trayvon Martin's name, and so, we keep writing to resist.

Marvel-worthy words from a twelve year old:

Watch your thoughts, because they become words.
Watch your words, because they become your actions.
Watch your actions, because they become your habits.
Watch your habits, because they become your character.
Watch your character, because it becomes your destiny.

In Indy, #blackyouthmatter.

HOW AN OLD WHITE GUY GOT WOKE

DAN WAKEFIELD

Almost sixty-five years ago, I covered the murder trial that helped trigger the Civil Rights movement. In the decades that followed, I befriended the iconic Black author James Baldwin. But it took returning home to Indianapolis in my eighties to fully appreciate the terrible injustice this country inflicts on its citizens of color.

Five years ago, a man called me and began with an apology. "I'm sure you get too many of these," he said. "But I have to call you because I am writing a book on the Emmett Till murder trial, and you are the only one who was at the trial and is still alive."

That has become my distinction.

The Supreme Court had outlawed school segregation in its 1954 decision *Brown v. Board of Education*, ruling that "separate but equal" education was not valid and no longer the law of the land. Everyone knew this was a major decision that would have a huge impact on American life. There was a feeling of national apprehension. What would happen? Would the South revolt? Would it be the start of another Civil War? It felt like the country was holding its breath.

A year later, in the summer of 1955, newspapers across the country reported the murder of a fourteen-year-old Black boy from Chicago. Emmett Till had gone to visit his great-uncle in Mississippi and was killed for allegedly whistling at a white woman. It was the first big "racial" story that followed the Supreme Court decision, and the trial of the two white men charged with the crime captivated the nation.

I had come to know Murray Kempton, a columnist for *The New York Post*, and I begged him to find me, then twenty-three years old, a way to go to Mississippi and write about the trial. My slim credentials at the time included summer reporting jobs at *The Indianapolis Star* and *The Grand Rapids Press*. I was an ambitious young journalist, and this trial would be historic. I felt I had to be there. Somehow, Kempton persuaded *The Nation* magazine to send me. My payment was a round-trip bus ticket from New York City to Sumner, Mississippi. The trip took two days and a night, stopping at every small burg on the way.

Reporters from all over the country had come to the tiny courthouse in the Mississippi Delta. The prosecutor made his case: Till had gone with some other boys to a small store in a town near Sumner. Supposedly, he whistled at or in some way flirted with the woman behind the counter. She complained to her husband, and he and a cousin went to Till's great-uncle's house that night and demanded "the boy from Chicago." Till came out, the two white men took him away, and his body was found a few days later at the bottom of the Tallahatchie River with a 70-pound cotton-gin fan tied around his neck. His face and his body were mutilated, and his mother insisted on an open-casket funeral "so people could see what they did to my boy."

The two murderers—they later sold their confessions to *Look* magazine— sat in the front row, smoking cigars, smiling, yawning. At the end of a week of testimony, the defense attorney announced his faith that "every last Anglo-Saxon one of you men in this jury has the courage to set these men free." It took the jury a little over an hour to do just that. The first sentence of my article for *The Nation*, titled "Justice in Sumner," captured the hopelessness of the decision: "The crowds are gone and this Delta town is back to its silent, solid life that is based on cotton and the proposition that a whole race of men was created to pick it."

I had no idea then that the story would be the beginning of a writing career and life that often orbited the Civil Rights movement. Over the next decade, I wrote several magazine features on the subject. A few years after the Till trial, I befriended the author James Baldwin, who became the twentieth century's most eloquent voice on the Black experience in America. But it wasn't until I moved back to Indianapolis in 2011 that I finally came to understand how ubiquitous racism remains, and what my experience in Sumner should have taught me long ago.

———————

I first met James Baldwin—Jimmy, as he was known to his friends—in 1957 at The White Horse Tavern, Greenwich Village's historic literary hangout. Recognizing the author from the photograph on the cover of his *Notes of a Native Son*, I walked over and introduced myself. The last sentence of his "Autobiographical Notes" in that book had sent a chill of inspiration through me, and I adopted it as my highest and most sacred goal: "I want to be an honest man and a good writer." I told him I was writing my first book, a journalistic account of Spanish Harlem (*Island in the City*), and he asked to read it, and invited me to his apartment on Horatio Street for bourbon and Bessie Smith records.

Jimmy knew I had covered the Till murder trial, and he quizzed me about it. He asked what the people in the town felt when the two men they knew were murderers were set free.

"That's the amazing thing, Jimmy," I said. "The people in the town were pleased; they thought it was right to let the killers go free."

Jimmy's great eyes fixed on me and he said something I will never forget:

"You mean the *white* people in the town."

I winced. *Of course*, I thought. He was teaching me to see more than I was trained to see through the shuttered lens of white perception. He was also an inspiration, continually supporting my work and encouraging me. Once, after he'd returned from a talk at Howard University, he said an old professor there had told him, "When you finish, you got to have a shelf of books, a whole shelf." He pointed his finger in my direction, and indicated he expected no less from me: "A shelf of books, baby, a whole shelf."

After years of friendship, I remember clearly the last time we got together. We were walking uptown on Seventh Avenue from the Village to Chelsea, without umbrellas, as the rain drenched us. Jimmy had been invited by his friend Mary Painter, a prominent economist, to have dinner with a woman she knew who was visiting from France. He asked me to come along. We arrived at Mary's apartment soaked and chilled, and she quickly got out the bourbon. The French woman—Francine, I'll call her—was very pleasant and drank along with us. The conversation started out general and light, with plenty of laughter. Then Jimmy began to speak of his younger sister, and his jovial mood quickly darkened. His sister was having a fashion show in Harlem a week later, and her future hopes were wrapped up in it. She was only sixteen, but she knew the odds were against her as a Black girl in Harlem. The leading fashion designers and stylists of the 1950s were all white, the models mostly blond-haired and blue-eyed. There was a "brown bag" standard of beauty in the business: If you were darker than a brown grocery-store bag, you didn't meet it.

"She is sixteen and she is suffering!" Jimmy said.

"Oh, Jimmy," Francine replied. "All sixteen-year-old girls suffer. I have a teenage sister myself, and she is suffering, too."

Stoked with bourbon and wine, I leaped in.

"Teenage boys suffer, too!" I said, thinking self-pityingly of my own adolescent agonies.

"People can only suffer to their own capacity for suffering," I added, imagining I had come up with some irrefutable gem of human understanding. Only Mary held her tongue that night. Jimmy sat on my left, and he turned his eyes to me with a look of disillusionment and rage. He didn't raise his voice as he spoke, which made his words even more terrible.

"You don't understand," he said.

The table was silent for the rest of the night.

I continued to follow Jimmy on television as he marched with Martin Luther King, confronted Bobby Kennedy, and ultimately moved to the south of France, where he died in 1987. I even reviewed his powerful book *The Fire Next Time* for *The New York Times*. But I never called him to try to get together again after that evening at Mary's. What could I say? I still didn't understand what had upset my friend so profoundly.

Of all places, Indianapolis seemed like an unlikely place for an awakening. I came back here to live in 2011 after decades in New York, L.A., and Miami—cities with more diverse populations. My friend Kurt Vonnegut once said of Indy, "I grew up in a city as segregated as Biloxi, Mississippi, except for the drinking fountains and the buses."

My own journey toward that revelation never would have happened had it not been for the annual Spirit & Place Festival. I was asked to give a speech at the event in 2015 when the theme was "Dreams." After my brief presentation on literary dreams, I stayed to hear a panel discussion on dreams for our city. The panelist whose thoughts I found most interesting was Phyllis Boyd, director of Groundwork Indy, which employs youth to upgrade public spaces. Boyd, a Black woman, said her dream was for "a city where everyone can contribute." My self-referential response was, *"Great, 'everyone' includes old guys!"*

I introduced myself to Boyd afterward, wanting to connect, to show my appreciation for her work, her effort to reach across the color gap. She had mentioned that her father had gone to Crispus Attucks, so I asked if she had seen the film *Something to Cheer About*, a documentary about the Crispus Attucks basketball team led by Oscar Robertson that won the state championship two years in a row (1955–1956) and became the first Black high school in America to win a state championship in any team sport. (Until 1942, Black high schools were prohibited from taking part in events of the Indiana High School Athletic Association.) The city re-routed the Attucks victory parade; after a brief stop at Monument Circle, the usual site of such gatherings, the team was whisked off to celebrate with its fans at a park in one of the city's Black neighborhoods. Robertson left the festivities early, depressed. He went home and told his father, "They don't want us."

Boyd said she hadn't seen it, so I told her I would mail her the DVD. I felt I had done my good deed for race relations.

Three weeks later, I was giving a talk on Jack Kerouac at Indy Reads Books, and Boyd showed up in the audience. She thanked me for the documentary and gave me a gift in return—a book I had been conscientiously avoiding since it had published earlier that year, *Between the World and Me*, by Ta-Nehisi Coates. A lot of people were comparing it to the work of James Baldwin, which made me feel defensive, as if I were a self-appointed "defender" of Jimmy's status as the nation's greatest Black author, even though he told me I didn't understand him.

Because the book had been given to me as a gift, I felt obligated to read it. *Between the World and Me* is in the form of a letter from Coates to his fifteen-year-old son, warning him of "the system that makes your body breakable." He tells his son that, "I am writing you because this was the year you saw Eric Garner choked to death for selling cigarettes; because you know now that Renisha McBride was shot for seeking help, and that John Crawford was shot down for browsing in a department store. And you have seen men in uniform drive by and murder Tamir Rice, a twelve-year-old child whom they were oathbound to protect. And you have seen men in the same uniforms pummel Marlene Pinnock, someone's grandmother, on the side of the road. And you know now, if you did not before, that the police departments of your country have been endowed with the authority to destroy your body."

Maybe Coates's words reached me on a level that Baldwin's hadn't because by then I, too, had seen the shootings of innocent Black men by police on television, over and over. I Googled "How many unarmed Black people were killed by police in 2015?" The answer was at least 104, nearly twice each week. I printed the names and pictures of those killed. Rayshaun, Lamontez, Christopher, Junior, Keith, Philandro, DeAngelo, Reginald— names representing recently living and breathing human beings whose skin was darker than mine, whose skin color made them "breakable."

I thought back to a WFYI documentary called *Indy in the '50s* that I had participated in a few years prior. One question asked of all of us who were here in that decade was, "What was it like to go downtown to the Circle when you were in high school?" I talked happily of what fun that was, how much my friends and I enjoyed it. The very next cut was of Robertson, the state's greatest high school basketball player and one of my heroes, saying, "We were afraid to go downtown."

I didn't know. I think of my friends and myself in those days as good, friendly, honest young people. It's easy to say now, but it's true: We would have been ashamed to know how our city and its police force discriminated against Black people. The evidence was all around us, of course. I graduated in 1950, before Robertson, but I saw his older brother, Bailey, play for Attucks. Those Attucks players were the only Black people I saw when I was growing up at the corner of 61st Street and Winthrop Avenue. Sumner, Mississippi, the site of the Emmett Till trial, was no more segregated than Broad Ripple.

In 2016, I was invited to a poetry reading on the south side of the city. Talented poets are plentiful here, but that night it felt as if one of them jumped off the stage and into our heads. Tasha Jones didn't merely read, but "performed" her poem—her whole body seemed to move and strain in an attempt to make us not only hear but absorb the words of her poem, "From Pyramids to Plantations to Projects to Penitentiaries."

Jones was also a teacher, and she invited me to visit her class of eighth-grade boys, most of whom are Black, at Tindley Preparatory Academy on the northeast side. Jones taught the boys the most appropriate (safest) way to respond if stopped by police—stand straight, hands out of pockets, clearly visible; speak only "Yes, sir" and "No, sir" to questions; if traveling in a group, re-form in twos. These are part of a Black American child's standard curriculum of safety and survival. We are not speaking of Black children from Chicago going to the Mississippi Delta in 1955, we are speaking of Black children here, now.

My racial education in Indy continued when I met Aleta Hodge, a fellow former writer for *The Shortridge Daily Echo*. She had just written a book called *Indiana Avenue: Life and Musical Journey from 1915–2015*. I first heard of Indiana Avenue as a boy, when I was told—as white boys in our city in those days often were—that Indiana Avenue was a dangerous place where dope-crazed Black men would cut the throat of any white person who entered. In the segregated white high schools of my era, it was traditional to "dare" a boy to drive his car down that street with his windows rolled down to see if he could make it through the alleged danger zone alive.

When I learned of this hometown lore as a child in the 1940s, I had no idea that my favorite musical group, The Ink Spots, whose hit record *If I Didn't Care* sold 19 million copies, got their start on Indiana Avenue. (One of their original members, Jerry Daniels, taught music at Attucks.) I didn't know that the strip was a legendary mecca of jazz, and a favorite stop on "The Chitlin' Circuit," the segregated entertainment route that went through Cleveland, Detroit, Indianapolis, Kansas City, Memphis, and New Orleans.

"Many people ask today," Hodge writes, "'Why didn't I know about Indiana Avenue?' Other cities have aggressively marketed their musical heritage. In fact, the city name is tied to the music such as Kansas City Blues or New Orleans Jazz. However, Indianapolis did not proclaim its musical heritage."

I suspect the reason those who ran this city in the middle of the twentieth century wanted to hide that history is because the musicians were Black. We've now been given five books on Indiana Avenue and its nationally acclaimed music. All five are by African American writers. Not a single white author I'm aware of has seen fit to cover this fascinating history.

From Hodge's book, I learned that Noble Sissle, a Black man who was born and grew up here, wrote *Shuffle Along*, the first Black musical on Broadway, in 1921, giving singer Paul Robeson and dancer Josephine Baker the first stage roles of their internationally famous careers. The musical was revived on Broadway four years ago and nominated for ten Tony Awards. Sissle wrote many other musicals and songs, including the national hit "I'm Just Wild About Harry." Oh yes, he also wrote "The Butler University War Song." Does his story not belong to the history of this city and state?

Beyond learning about the rich musical tradition of Indiana Avenue, I also found Hodge's descriptions of everyday Black life in Indy enlightening. These nuggets are what white people call "Black history." In reality, it is Indiana history, American history. In a section on the plague of tuberculosis in the early twentieth century, a neighbor tells the author's grandmother, Estella Hodge, about the closing of the only clinic that accepted Black patients. The community panics. In another passage, Hodge describes the drainage problems, flooding, and mosquito populations near the White River and Fall Creek during that era. "Due to these inferior conditions," she writes, "colored people were only allowed to live in this segregated community."

Segregation has a history as ugly here as in the Deep South. A Black family named Greer owned acres of land near 64th Street and Grandview Drive, and according to Hodge, "sold parcels of land to their fellow Attucks alumni. It became a middle-class, suburban neighborhood with the nickname 'the golden ghetto.' The homeowners were denied mortgages by local banks, and had to obtain financing from out-of-state companies." Hodge's family and their neighbors couldn't get a mortgage in Indiana. Citizens who had been here for generations had to get mortgages from banks in Colorado.

That kind of discrimination effectively walled off the Black population into urban ghettos. "White flight" shifted Indy's Caucasian population to Carmel, Greenfield, and elsewhere. For the Black community, the results were disastrous. My friend Jimmy summed up the phenomenon back in the 1960s: "Real-estate values don't go down when I move in; they go down when you move out."

———

Jimmy, I think I finally get it. I think I'm beginning to understand. I may not be fully "woke," but at least I am blinking and rubbing my eyes. Absorbing this information about my hometown, these should-have-been-obvious examples of the vast and unceasing injustice this country inflicts on its citizens of color, I look back on your work. What rings most true to me is your story *Sonny's Blues*, about a jazz musician. It describes the music of the group as it reaches a peak:

"Creole [the bass player] stepped forward to remind them that what they were playing was the blues. He hit something in all of them, he hit something in me, myself, and the music tightened, and deepened, apprehension began to beat the air. Creole began to tell us what the blues were all about. They were not about anything very new. He and his boys up there were keeping it new, at the risk of ruin, destruction, madness, and death, in order to find new ways to make us listen. For, while the tale of how we suffer and how we are delighted and how we may triumph is never new, it always must be heard."

Why did I hear it here when I had missed it so many other places? Maybe the truth learned on the home ground is more real to us. When I witnessed the Till trial all those years ago, I assumed that racism was a regional problem, not a national one. Learning the history of my hometown—that Blacks weren't welcome downtown when I was in high school, that they hadn't been allowed in tuberculosis centers here or their doctors in our hospitals until 1954—felt personal, not abstract.

In the course of this journey, I realized that when Jimmy lamented his sixteen-year-old sister's suffering, he didn't just mean the barriers she faced as a Black woman in a segregated fashion world. He meant the ongoing dangers, handicaps, and injustices that are part of life for African Americans in this country. Not long after our last dinner together, Baldwin was beaten up at an Irish bar in Greenwich Village because he was sitting with two white friends, one of them a blond woman.

Racism is systemic, but grasping the injustice of it is individual. For me, it took listening to Phyllis Boyd talk about her dreams for our city and getting to know her as she drove me around the underserved neighborhoods where she works. It took hearing Tasha Jones perform her poem and observing the lesson she gave her eighth graders on how to be safe as young Black boys today. It took reading Aleta Hodge's book on Indiana Avenue and learning not only about my hometown's great musical heritage, but also about what our local Black citizens have suffered. The revelation was not that bigotry once existed in some far-off place, but that it's a daily terror Black people here continue to survive.

RECLAMATION

SARAH LAYDEN

A boy and a girl stand on opposite sides of falling-down 29th Street, where new construction means sheets of plywood covering broken windows. Nature dictates the local beautification projects: prickly vines twining through loose siding. Reclamation.

The preteens run this neighborhood, now that the adults have given up on it. These young ones herd themselves in groups of no fewer than five, no more than ten. The boy and the girl, emissaries of their respective packs, edge closer to the curb, apart from the others. They wait for me. Mine is the last car in a stream of traffic. I am what stands between them on this near-Northside Indy one-way street.

They were children too long ago; they are still children. Pink blush shades her pudgy cheeks. Her ladies own the south side of the street. They wear their jeans tight, their hair braided and piled like small, impenetrable mazes atop their heads. Their new bras and what's beneath strain against snug T-shirts. They tug the cotton prints away from their stomachs one moment, arching their backs the next.

The boy's Indiana Pacers jersey hangs loose (I think of the time I asked my sister-in-law for her fourteen-year-old's shirt size one Christmas: "He's either a Small Adult or a Large Child"). He hunkers on his corner with the males, their too-large clothing hiding collective bony elbows and knees. They tease the girls in that way particular to siblings and middle school-ers—love-infused gestures of hate in the form of shouted insults, crude hand signals, whatever can be expressed at a safe distance. Their energy frightens adults, parents, and teachers who are tired from life. The preteens will never be tired, even if they stay up all night when no one tells them to go to bed.

Sneakers dangle from telephone wires, straining the laces. I read it in the newspaper: Police say the hanging shoes mean a drug house is near. On this street, it could be the one with the boarded windows, a black X spray-painted on either side of the front door, like the cartoon equivalent of dead eyes. Or the house eaten by fire, still charred around the edges, where children play tag on a dandelion-and-dirt front lawn.

The boy holds a bag in his hands. Before my car has safely passed, he and the girl begin walking towards each other, quick but unhurried. In the rearview I anticipate the handoff of meth, crack, whatever comes from these closed homes. A few yards from my rear bumper, the pair meets atop the dotted white line in the middle of the street. They touch hands briefly, then part as if dancing, pushing off one another, retreating to their own corners. In her hands, his offering: a bag of gummy worms, a fat sack of rainbow-hued candy.

Gummy worms laced with crack, my husband might joke over tonight's dinner. But I am still several miles from home. The kids are growing distant in my mirror. Behind me, the street gives way to the ruined homes, and before the sky opens and expands in the small rectangle through which I view their lives, I see the pair of dirty sneakers hanging from the telephone wires. Maybe it's the work of some drug lord, spiting the police. Or maybe it was some Large Child or Small Adult, a kid willing to part with a bag of gummy worms, who launched his own shoes upward. The impulse and sacrifice of it. After all, who are we to keep flight to ourselves?

TRANSPO

THEON LEE

It's a bunch of us never traveling by interstate
We enter states of commute and communion, and honestly/
Taking the high road isn't always a promise for solid ground
Yeah, that exit's cute, but execute incorrectly watch that windshield become an ejection chute/
But that's beside the point,
Beneath the overpass,
Our path progresses slowly, and pulls over fast/
"Stop"
"Requested"
Passenger 22 barely lifts his feet from the pavement, commits to a stumble as he boards the 39/
Most affectionately known as the "Dirty Nine"/
First one to make to Mitthoeffer, last one to turn east at Meridian/
All it would take is a broken MPC and a sax player, and it would be a regular juke joint on wheels/
You can find squares, shots, and pills/
Syringes, mixtapes, and thrills/
Maybe even some incense/
Maybe they confront your innocence, and in defense remove the bright smiles from your face, and tell you to replace them with a touchscreen, earphones, and your head down for the next thirty minutes/
"Stop"
"Requested"
The 19 feels like a field trip,
Then a housing tour,
Then a city bus,
Then a "thank God, I thought I missed it"/
I used to work out in Castleton,
My boss/father in law would talk about how there are quartermillion dollar houses up the street, and no other jiffy lube should compete,
And the air would smell sweet, then soot/
Then sweat/
Then sales/

Them smells,
Become their own bus line into reflection,
"Stop"
"Requested"
Stop requesting
Another bus, like they fall from the sky when you miss yours/
Stop requesting
Another bus stop, closer to the crib
Stop requesting
Benches, shelters, sidewalks
Fewer gas stations,
More grocery stores
They got four within a five-mile radius of monument circle/
But got negative one double 8 on Central
Stop asking for a ride/
Red line is as sufficient as it can get,
That's why it had to be revived/
We've got nature trails in places where ain't no sidewalk/
And should you get tagged, they'll have the nerve to spray paint your
means of transpo,
Same color as the folks who love for us to pose for their brochures, but
wish that we would
Stop requesting/
Stop requesting/
"Stop Requested"/
It's a bunch of us never traveling by interstate
We enter states of commute and communion, and honestly/
Taking the high road isn't always a promise for solid ground…

FOUNTAIN FOSSIL

MANÒN VOICE

2019 was the year of the Red Line.
The year Indianapolis grew legs, spider veins of bus routes,
Stretch marking into Fountain Square, officially gentrified.

It was the year Peppy Grill, almost 70,
Bought a facelift of brick wall, a plasma TV,
Lambid lighting and a liquor license.

2019 was the year that Chreece Festival received a grant from CICF,
Talib Kweli performed at Radio Radio,
And hip-hop was legitimized in Indianapolis.

It was the year Bovacanti Coffee took
On the namesake of a former mom and pop
Grocer, disappeared under a new era of national chains.

2019 was the year we caroused over the goodbye of Grove Haus,
Now listed as permanently closed
On Google.

2019 was also the year that Julie—
58, homeless, beloved of Fountain Square,
Was found murdered in St. Patrick's church.

It was the same year, Dennis, her husband,
Also homeless, was killed months earlier,
Pedestrian in a multiple vehicle collision.

2019 was the year that their friend Tommy sat on a curb
And passed away behind the new bus stop.
The memorial ground of his leaving, littered with liquor bottles, allowed
for a month.

2019 was the same year I stopped seeing Ron
Outside of Sunday morning mass on Prospect Street,
Fastened to a change bucket atop his amputated limbs.

It was the year I stopped hearing
Drunken shouts
Boomerang off the fountainheads in the square

And the row of open faces of harmless hurts
Line the aluminum colored benches
In front of the PNC Bank on Virginia Avenue.

That year, winter paid its first tithe
The 11th day of November.
I try to forgive its chewing mouth, its compost that will turn bodies into
rose buds and lilies.

GROWING FOOD IN THE CITY: URBAN AGRICULTURE AND COMMUNITY GARDENS IN INDIANAPOLIS

ANGELA HERRMANN

"Urban planners and agricultural experts predict that there will be no farmland remaining in [Marion County] by the year 2050."
—William D. Dalton, *The Encyclopedia of Indianapolis*

The 2020 gardening season began in late January, much like it has each year for the past two decades, with a few messages back and forth among gardeners with offers of catalog and seed exchanges and attempts to schedule a time to meet and organize ourselves for the upcoming season. As one of the original members of the Rocky Ripple Burkhart Community Garden, established in 2001, our routine has evolved from email messages (and a short-lived newsletter) to a now-defunct Yahoo group, to a now-active Facebook group.

But by mid-March 2020, the COVID-19 pandemic had nearly shuttered the entire city of Indianapolis except for those businesses and services deemed essential. Nevertheless, we were quick to establish that a community garden is essential, as long as those working in the garden followed masking and social distancing guidelines.

That's the alchemy of community gardens. No matter what life throws at Hoosiers, such as war, economic uncertainty, social inequality, energy shortages, insect pests, or even a pandemic, community gardens always will be essential. Even while social distancing, gardeners will transform a piece of land into a vibrant oasis of community, food, and flowers. Rocky Ripple's community gardeners are part of a rich tradition of Indianapolis residents who have grown food in the city.

Indeed, people have always grown food in or near cities. For instance, in the 1850s, "prior to refrigerated transport, New York City supplied all its food for a population of over a million from within 7 miles of the borders of the city...?"[1] Community gardens have been an integral part of U.S. urban food production with their historical roots emerging from England's allotment movement in response to urbanization and industrialization in the late 1700s and 1800s.

The Roots of Urban Food in Indianapolis

Food production has always been a critical component of Indiana's economy. Indiana established the State Board of Agriculture in 1851 to promote "modern" farming. The first Indiana State Fair was held in 1852 to promote agriculture throughout the state. And in 1862, Congress passed the Morrill Act, which established a nationwide chain of land grant colleges and universities to teach agricultural and mechanical arts—the Extension Program. Purdue University, Indiana's land grant school, was founded in 1869 to help farmers learn new methods, adopt new technologies, and increase production. Little did they know that Purdue University Extension would later become a vital partner to Indianapolis's urban growers with the same objectives!

Indianapolis's earliest pioneer and immigrant farmers took advantage of central Indiana's alluvial soils, enriched by the White River and its tributaries. On higher ground, directly across the river from Rocky Ripple, long before Rocky Ripple was incorporated and long before Crows Nest became one of Indianapolis's poshest neighborhoods, the Lemings were one of the families who farmed the area. Tombstones for my fourth great-grandparents, Indiana pioneers James and Nancy (Thomas) Hubbartt and other Hubbartt relatives, are located on what was once Leming land. James had farmed near Broad Ripple and near Crooked Creek east of Michigan Road.

Better known are the German immigrant farmers who arrived in Indianapolis by the mid-1800s. You might recognize some of these names: Brehob, Nordholt, Hohlt, and Heidenreich. They provided fresh fruits and vegetables for more than 15,000 Civil War soldiers in Indianapolis (perhaps James Hubbartt's son and my third great grandfather George was among them?). They organized themselves as the Deutscher Gartner Unterstützungs Verein zu Indianapolis or Farmers Benefit Society of Indianapolis in 1867.

These immigrant farmers sold their produce at the original Indianapolis City Market, an open-air structure from the 1830s through the mid-1880s. The current Indianapolis City Market opened in 1886 and served farmers from within and around the city.

1 David Blume, "Food and Permaculture," accessed June 19, 2020, www.permaculture.com/node/141.

In 1920, the Marion County Greenhouse Growers Association formed to promote uniform growth of produce. According to Dawn Mitchell in her *Indianapolis Star* article "Retro Indy: The Greenhouse Growers," by the 1940s, "...the south side—most notably along Bluff Road—had the highest concentration of greenhouses in the United States with 80 to 85 growers owning nearly 40 acres each."

Of course, if you know the topography of Indianapolis, with the exception of Crows Nest, flooding has always been a concern. Rocky Ripple gardeners have always been acutely aware of this possibility, but they're not the only ones, as this newspaper article about Tom Taggart's levee from the May 24, 1891, issue of the *Indianapolis Journal* attests.

TOM TAGGART'S LEVEE.

An Unpromising Strip of Land Turned Into a Vegetable and Colorado Beetle Garden.

The name of County Auditor Taggart is attaching itself to a landmark to which it may endure to the last moment of recorded time unless the turbulent flood of White river washes it off. Some time ago Mr. Taggart bought about two hundred low-lying acres immediately south of the Belt road, the Bluff gravel road forming the boundary line on the east and White river's sandy marge on the west. The soil is rich as Jersey cream, but at any time a slight rise in the river rolls a flood over it which, while adding to its fertility, gives no security to crop-raising. Beside this the wash of waters was eating away the acres. Mr. Taggart, having bought this unpromising strip of land, is now making it valuable by building a levee 2,300 feet long, which, as it grows under the labor directed by Wm. Wishard, contractor, bears the name, "Tom Taggart's levee." Mr. Taggart is receiving instructions in garden farming, and has growing on this strip thirty acres of peas, several acres of corn, tomatoes, cabbage and beans, the greater part of the ground being given up to potatoes. The Colorado beetle, in considerable numbers, has appeared in this potato patch, and he offers all the bugs that that anybody may want as fish-bait to any one who will come and pick them.

Urban Food Supports War Efforts

While many Hoosiers aspired to get off the farm and into the city, it seems that the farm never really left Indianapolis residents. The farms that weren't developed or paved over, the city simply grew around them. Larger scale food production evolved with the times, and yet backyard and community gardens became essential to the WWI and WWII efforts. Urban food production meant transportation resources could be conserved to support the war.

WWI War Gardens

So many Indianapolis residents participated in War Gardens that Indiana became home to one of the largest state campaigns of the National War Garden Commission. Not surprisingly, a Purdue University lecturer coordinated that effort. Indianapolis banks and businesses helped distribute the "Food Garden Primer" for the benefit of those who did not have growing experience.

"The women of Indiana surely have a big campaign mapped out and the national war garden commission will be very glad to help them in every way…. For Indianapolis alone we have sent 10,000 of our primers to… the Patriotic Gardeners Association," according to a report appearing in the March 8, 1918, issue of the *Indianapolis News*. Even the real estate industry promoted the effort. 1920s advertisements promoted homeownership as a means of owning a war garden.

WWII Victory Gardens

Within a generation, gardens were again essential to wartime efforts, such that rationing of canned food required everyone to participate in food production. The 1943 Victory Garden program called for four types of gardens: farm gardens, city home gardens, school gardens, and community gardens. In 1943 alone, Marion County's Victory Gardens produced 40% of all vegetables grown. Even Indianapolis's *Jewish Post* promoted more participation in the effort and encouraged a 15% increase in production.

Post-War Food Production

As post-war prosperity pushed food production away from cities, including Indianapolis, grocers rather than gardeners emerged as key food providers. While expendable income grew for many, not everyone shared in the postwar prosperity. Thus, projects like the Flanner House Urban Farm helped address high costs and food insecurity for African American residents.

Albert A. Moore, director of agriculture, launched urban farming efforts at Flanner House in 1946 after having served in Camp Atterbury in WWII. Flanner House launched a cannery in 1947 to address increased food prices and shortages. The cannery and gardens were originally located at 812 N. West Street. According to the Indiana Historical Society, the Flanner House community tended some 600 community garden plots. At the same time, members trained to can produce and sell staples at a co-op grocery store.

Community Gardens and Urban Food Production: Responses to Hunger

Community gardening regained its popularity in the United States again during the late 1960s through the 1980s, during the Vietnam conflict, and following the 1979 oil crisis. A pattern suggests that community gardening and urban farming activities have tended to increase during periods of war or social uncertainty. When the economy contracts, people rely on gardening as a way to stretch their food budgets.

Mayor's Garden Project

The Mayor's Garden Project, organized under the administration of Mayor Richard Lugar on April 5, 1975, was launched in response to rising food prices. Lugar saw the value in urban gardening when he learned that "a person farming a 15-by-18-foot lot could raise $100 worth of food during the summer."[2] According to the inflation calculator, that translates to about $476.57 today.

The first garden, created to aid poor and older adults, was located on land at Central State Hospital. The city leased plots for $5 ($1 for senior citizens), and provided six kinds of seeds and tomato plants, along with horticultural advice. Inner-city residents were given access to garden plots to rent. Because of the popularity of the program, with 3,000 people signing up for the project within two weeks, more land was added to the project, including 20 acres in the 2400 block of north Tibbs on Indianapolis's west side.

Phyllis Hackett, former president of Riverside Neighborhood, Inc. and former planner for Community Action Against Poverty (C.A.A.P.) in the 1970s, said city employee Mary Oldham "garnered the idea" of a city-wide gardening program. Hackett took the idea to a city director who allowed her to organize a C.A.A.P. neighborhood gardening program, which she

---

2 *Indianapolis Star,* "City Eyes Garden Aid," March 6, 1975.

said contributed to the launching of the Mayor's Garden Project (Hackett). Gleaners Food Bank was another outcome of C.A.A.P. (later renamed Community Action of Greater Indianapolis). Gleaners incorporated in 1980, expanding from Marion County to serve the state of Indiana, creating one of the nation's first affiliate food bank networks.

Capital City Garden Project

In 1985, Indianapolis became the site of one of 23 urban gardening programs funded by the U.S. Department of Agriculture. The Indianapolis program was administered by the Purdue University Cooperative Extension Service in Marion County as the Capital City Garden Project. The Capital City Garden Project's mission was to be a community-based educational program in Marion County, promoting healthy people and greener neighborhoods through gardening. The project provided neighborhood groups and backyard gardeners the basics of urban food production and neighborhood beautification. The CCGP, once affiliated with the American Community Garden Association, has now been rolled into other Extension programming.

City-Wide Garden Projects

In the late 1980s to early 1990s, Purdue Extension began establishing gardening projects at public housing sites and inner-city neighborhoods in Indianapolis. Roots of Ruckle, which was located in the Mapleton Fall Creek neighborhood, was among the first. In 1990, longtime Beechwood Gardens resident Essie Rowley, along with her neighbors, brought the nationwide project, End World Hunger Community Food Garden Club, to her eastside low-income public housing complex as a means of reducing hunger, eliminating crime, and improving residents' health. Rowley started the only community garden and the first food pantry in Indianapolis public housing with support from the Capital City Garden Project. Consequently, she was recognized in 1993 with the Mayor's Volunteer Partnership Award by then-mayor Stephen Goldsmith. John Shaughnessy documented her efforts in *The Indianapolis Star*, "Public Housing Matron Never Gives up Despite Life's Downs," October 8, 1993.

Indy's Community Gardens

When Tom Tyler began his work at Purdue Extension in 1988, community gardens happened mostly in public housing or near economically depressed areas. Tyler said he wanted to promote the idea that community gardens could be as diverse as those planting them: from a couple of people planting flowers, to large public garden plots and youth programs.

Indeed, community gardens seemed to sprout all over Indianapolis, at schools, churches, the Indianapolis Children's Museum, the governor's residence, Washington Park North Cemetery, and the Indiana Women's Prison. Tyler and his staff developed partnerships with the Marion County Health Department, schools, Indy Parks, community centers, the Knights of Columbus, Indianapolis Downtown, Inc., the Junior League, and Keep Indianapolis Beautiful to develop and promote community gardens. One outcome was the partnership between the Junior League and the Extension office to produce the publication *Neighborhood Harvest Building Community Gardens in Indianapolis*.

In 1997, when Governor Frank O'Bannon and his wife Judy moved into the governor's residence, First Lady O'Bannon immediately opened the residence gardens to the public, referring to them as an extension of the "state's living room."

In an interview with Mrs. O'Bannon, she said that when she and her husband lived on the Old Northside, they lived between two Housing and Urban Development (HUD) houses and among about 50 [neighborhood] kids. So, as Mrs. O'Bannon had done all of her life (growing up helping her mother in a Victory Garden), she "started digging around that lot, and soon the children began to come out, curious to see what she was doing. Shortly after the parents followed and before long, people who barely knew each other began getting to know each other and building trust." When the O'Bannons moved into the governor's residence, she continued promoting community gardening. When the ACGA national meeting came to Indianapolis in 1997, Mrs. O'Bannon served as the keynote speaker to some 300 attendees who also toured Indianapolis-area gardens.

The concept of food security became part of the Indianapolis community gardening landscape since many gardening projects emerged in response to limited access to fresh produce, high food prices, and hunger. In 1997 the Extension office partnered with Gleaners Food Bank and Americorps to develop a community food security coalition to create a foundation for increasing food access in what we now know as food deserts.

The Future of Food is in the City

That brings us to 2000, when Nancy Barton, Sue Gilfoy, and others began conversations around the launch of a community garden in Rocky Ripple's

Hohlt Park, on a site named in honor of market farmer Rick Burkhart who once owned the parcel of land on which the community garden is now located. The garden began its first season in 2001 and has enjoyed support from Purdue Extension and Keep Indianapolis Beautiful. It has been continuously active every year since. And while it's a relative newcomer in the city's urban agriculture efforts, nothing has changed. Gardener interest waxes and wanes depending on social pressures. Heavy precipitation events leave gardeners worried if this will be the year of the next big flood. And this year, for whatever reason, the Colorado beetles have staked a claim to the potato patches in several gardener plots, mine included. New this year is the pandemic, but that didn't stop Indianapolis-area gardeners from getting outside. Indeed, during a time of enforced quarantines, the community garden is the one place where we're never alone.

Meanwhile, a host of Indianapolis's young urban farmers now produce food to sell at markets and to restaurants—Matthew Jose and Amy Matthews have moved their farm to the Bluff Road area to rejuvenate one of the old German farmsteads along Bluff Road. To this day, gardeners continue to work the soil at the Mayor's Garden Plots on Tibbs. Flanner House, now located at 24th & Martin Luther King Street, continues its agricultural traditions to create one of the city's largest urban farms in the middle of a food desert. Albert Moore's descendent family members are carrying on the urban ag tradition in Mapleton Fall Creek. And now new communities of Burmese immigrants are establishing their roots in Indianapolis with new community gardens on the north and south sides of Indianapolis. At this rate, I'm confident that Indianapolis residents will continue gardening, and farming, in Marion County well into the future!

EIGHT GARDENS: ON GARDENING AS SOCIAL PRACTICE

KEVIN McKELVEY

One

I spent the first summer of my life, and every summer until I was eighteen, working and playing in my grandma Margaret's garden, on a rise in the till plains of central Indiana. It took up about a third of her two-acre barn lot in southwest Tipton County, the first place she and my granddaddy Lee ever owned after a lifetime farming others land. The northeastern corner started along the edge of the road, a few paces south of the driveway, and continued a hundred feet or so across to the old chicken coop. On the western edge, a strawberry patch thrived for years, and on the east side of the garden, her rows of sweet corn began, eight across, and ran south and then turned west, expanding to twenty-four, along the property line. The chicken coop marked the border between vegetable garden and sweet corn, and the corn rows curved around the tool shed to end at the neighbor's field, more than three hundred feet from their beginning.

There in the main garden—framed by sweet corn and strawberries—we grew zucchini, green beans, tomatoes, potatoes, sweet potatoes, onions, beets, broccoli, cauliflower, cabbage, and peppers. When my young consciousness sparked to memory and awareness, what I remember is that exquisite dirt, the strawberry patch, and the asparagus, rhubarb, struggling peach, and ancient apple tree by the house. All created tastes of wonder for eight-year-old me. I felt free, in control, at peace.

We planted on weekends in May after her neighbor, Don, disked the garden and planted her sweet corn. My grandma took care of hoeing and watering and more planting when we weren't there. My parents, Bob and Sue, my sister, Lee Anne, and I weeded and hoed and roto-tilled all summer, then picked and picked and picked, in awe of a fresh green bean or newly dug potato or a bright cherry tomato, eating as many strawberries as we picked, letting nothing go to waste. In that soil as good as any on the planet, I experienced gardening as a social practice, undertaken in coordination and collaboration with family and neighbors.

My grandma's devotion to sweet corn inspired our own, and the fact that almost every year in Tipton County is a good year for corn. When it came on, when all the kernels filled out and were still soft, we filled every container we had—old seed bags, little red wagons, garden carts, vegetable hampers, bushel baskets—in the morning before the heat. Under the shade of a silver maple, while the humidity rose and the wind picked up, we shucked ears and stacked them upright in plastic tubs. During and after lunch, my mom and grandma tonged corn into boiling water in big aluminum pots, which we called stirrers, to cook for a few minutes. They removed the ears and dropped them into an ice bath in the sink to stop the cooking. Once cooled, my grandmother ran each ear over a corn cutter a few times to remove the kernels, then we spooned the corn into bags to freeze.

This private family tradition was public in two ways. The first was the corn we froze by the quart in August and took to every pitch-in and pot-luck and family gathering and holiday from September to July. We put up enough to sustain us the year, usually more than fifty quarts; one year we froze just over a hundred. If there was any constant in my life, this was it, as reliable and regular as the sun. We thawed it out, then heated it in the microwave with a stick of butter or margarine and some salt. I ate at least two servings every time I could, a sugary reward.

And every bountiful August, when we grew more than we could eat or preserve ourselves, we filled the truck after supper with the extra ears and vegetables. We always made a delivery to Mrs. Wainwright, the retired principal who first gave my dad a teaching job, and made other stops on the way from my grandma's house between Tipton and Sheridan to our house near Lebanon. In the dark, we pulled up to friends' houses and gave away corn and other vegetables under the limited truck bed light. We doubled or tripled the number they asked for, in case the ears were small or bug-eaten or not filled out, and because we had so much. If they weren't home, we left a bag or two on their doorstep.

But this commerce was not sold. When I wanted to sell extra ears and tomatoes, my grandma rebuffed it with talk of insurance and liability. We grew what we needed and gave away the rest.

Grandma Margaret's death, the year I turned eighteen, shattered this idyll. We planted a garden at her house for a couple seasons, but it wasn't the same. In the twenty-three years since her death, I have been untethered from that profound experience—social and familial, collaborative and judicious, public and private—and I have been trying to recreate it.

Two

Seven years after my grandma's death, and five years after we let her garden return to grass and rented out her house and helped various friends with their gardens so we could have vegetables, my mom died. Any sort of knowledge, remembrance, intuition, know-how, this-is-how-we-did-it-this-one-year about the garden vanished. She knew how long to blanch the corn, simmer the green beans, stew the tomatoes. We were left to look for recipe cards she had memorized and find canning instructions on the internet.

My dad, sister, and I cemented our gardening with our neighbors, Lester and Joyce, about half a mile down the road from our house near Lebanon. They had retired from farming, sold most of their land, and built a modular house on a small triangle of land that had previously been their sweet corn patch and pig pasture. The new garden, with a rectangle of vegetables and a square of sweet corn, was a collaboration: they supplied the land, we supplied some labor, and we all had fresh food. During this time, I lived in Carbondale, Illinois, for graduate school, commuting back and forth on occasion.

Lester and Joyce had been farming and gardening this land for decades. Joyce always grew okra and orange tomatoes. Lester was a savant with corn, and he planted it to sell it. My dad fell into this commerce, and I helped when I could. They had a little under an acre of sweet corn near Lebanon, and sometimes one or two acres of sweet corn at their farm in Big Springs to the northeast. Every year, we filled truck beds with corn, selling it from Lester and Joyce's house along the road, dropping off orders of dozens of ears so people could boil and freeze it. One year, early on, I filled my car trunk with corn and drove it back to Carbondale to give away to friends and teachers.

When I moved back to Indiana and anchored myself in my old triangle—bordered by Indianapolis, Kokomo, and Lafayette—I created new routes for delivering extra vegetables to college friends and to new friends in Indianapolis. I enrolled in Purdue Extension's Master Gardener course to begin to relearn what I never knew in the first place. Later, I took my wife, Lakshmi, and my young children to pick and fill our minivan with corn, giving them the experience of the endless rows, the scratchy leaves, a preponderance of ears and good eating. When Lester died, his wisdom around timing the fertilizer and atrazine was lost, and my dad and I have never quite figured it out.

Three and Four

At the first house my wife and I shared in Indianapolis, a small cottage built after the Civil War, I carved out a small garden in the landscaping—

enough room for a few tomato plants, mostly harvested by the possums and rats. At our next house, a couple blocks south in the neighborhood, I was more ambitious, planning a raised bed by the house, three other raised beds along the fence, and plots of strawberries, raspberries, and blackberries. I shoveled out and hauled away the old dirt, full of lead and trash, tired from a century of use, and replaced it with new soil, compost, and peat. I built the raised beds out of cedar, and planted berries of all sorts outside the beds.

For all that work, we didn't have enough space to really produce and grow. But my children could eat berries directly from the plant, filling their mouths, rarely bringing any indoors to eat later.

Five

In late 2010, Jim Walker, my friend and collaborator at Big Car Collaborative, found a vacant tire center near Indianapolis's Lafayette Square Mall—a dying mall I went to a lot as a kid. The building sat along Lafayette Road, one of the busiest in the city. Jim's vision was to activate it as an arts and culture community center with some kind of garden or green space on the parking lot. Over the course of that first winter, I worked with Jim and other artists, including Zach Shields, Nathan Monk, and Tom Streit, to plan the garden. We wanted bright and colorful fruits and vegetables, thinking of them more like sculptures than food. We found models in other cities, figured out how to adapt them to our lot, and then ordered a trailer of hay bales, multiple loads of wood chips, and dump truck loads of mushroom compost.

We learned a lot about managing a public garden as we figured out how to grow on a parking lot along a busy, six-lane street. In the second year, Tom Streit and LaShawnda Crowe Storm did all kinds of work to increase the garden's impact. We gave away the food. We surprised visitors with black cherry tomatoes, got some chickens, started canning the food in glass jars. Some folks were picking their weekly vegetables for their family in the garden, and we were doing a little bit for food security in the neighborhood. The garden became an educational tool and spawned an additional garden space, north of the mall, run by an immigrant group.

This is where I started to realize the differences between a public garden and a private one. The Service Center garden was available to anyone twenty-four hours a day—hell, maybe people stopped by after the strip club across the street closed at three in the morning. The small beds in my backyard were only available to my family, and we had a measure of control. But a public garden can't be managed as easily—volunteers pull up flowers or rows, harvest too much, step on plants, which leads to a certain amount of chaos. I like the chaos more than the control. The tinkering, the variables, the testing of new ideas, just to see what will work.

After three years, our free lease at Service Center ended because a tenant wanted to pay full price for the building. Our soil was just getting productive, and we were finally beginning to understand it. I had again lost something I had helped build and create, something bigger than myself. Most of the soil went to Indy Urban Acres on the eastside, a market garden and a city park run by Tyler Gough and the Indianapolis Parks Foundation. Indy Urban Acres gives away one hundred percent of its vegetables and funds itself through flower production and plant sales, so I get to visit my organic matter from time to time.

Six

When Service Center ended in 2014, my home beds and berries were entering their best production, though the slugs liked to take one bite out of each ripe strawberry, and the neighbor's tree was shading out my beds along the fence. That same year, while my grandma's house in Tipton County was between renters, my family and I drove up there so my kids could run around and see the place as I remember it. I led Lakshmi to the southeast corner, where grandma Margaret's garden had been. I held out my arms at right angles and said, "This is what I mean when I say garden."

"Oh," she said. "I see now."

We had always had the vague idea of moving out to the country around Indianapolis or the woods north of Bloomington. But we had three children and jobs in Indianapolis. So, in 2017, we bought an acre and a half on the north side of Indianapolis with an old-growth forest in the front yard. I am working to take out some landscaping and add the garden I've always wanted. I just planted pecans and shagbark hickories in the front yard, and I will add pawpaws and persimmons in the fall, maybe some blueberries then or next year, to create my own food forest.

Last year, with part of a Creative Renewal grant from the Arts Council of Indianapolis, I ordered every seed I ever wanted. I spent $230 on a broadfork and $60 on a stirrup hoe. I bought fluorescent lights and grow trays so I could grow starts in the basement on the wire shelf the previous owner had left. In the front yard, I built a permaculture bed of asparagus and strawberries. The strawberries grew and sent out shoots, and the asparagus flowered on their alien-looking stalks. I weeded a couple times, but the weeds did not grow like in the backyard garden, and I harvested nothing in anticipation of this year.

Now, my asparagus and strawberry patch is thriving, a little shrine to my grandma Margaret. I'm getting so much asparagus this year we can't possibly eat it all. I posted on social media to see if anyone wanted some, and more than twenty people responded. I may not get to them all this year, but I've begun to figure out a distribution plan. I remember our old vegetable and corn route, from my grandma's house to ours. My grandma kept her list of neighbors and friends in her head. I have my own list now.

Seven

Last year, I convinced my dad to roto-till the plot the renters gardened in on my grandma Margaret's property and plant pumpkins and melons. We used to call the place grandma's house, but the house itself caught fire in 2017, and we had to demolish it—now the property is just the two acres with a gambrel barn and other outbuildings in need of repair. The weeds overtook the melons in the plot, but the pumpkins grew well enough for us to take home dozens.

Even if there isn't a house there, I still see that birth patch as a place to engage friends and neighbors in the public practice of gardening. I always wanted to keep the house as a writing studio and a place for visiting writers and artists. And now melons and pumpkins can be our public practice. Last year, my dad and his girlfriend brought her grandkids up for hot dogs and s'mores and pumpkin picking. My family and I went another day and had enough to take home to share. This year, we can share with neighbors there. Maybe we can invite some friends up to pick pumpkins as well.

I have never understood how to make money gardening and farming, although I know many market farmers in Indianapolis who do it. I have worked and learned on the farms of Amy Matthews and Matthew Jose of Mad Farmers Collective. Danial Garcia of Garcia's Gardens will tell me anything I want to know.

But I guess I still don't know enough, and the work interests me not as business, but as art and creative practice. I remember my grandma's labor and knowledge, having enough of everything to share, and the process that can sustain a place and its people.

Eight

I teach writing and social practice art at the University of Indianapolis. My work and teaching have always been inspired by places, by the dirt of that rise in Tipton County. Service-learning is integral to many of my courses, including my Urban Food and Farming Spring Term course. Last time I taught it, we served and learned on four farms around Indianapolis. This time, after years of asking, we were given two university-owned lots on which to build a garden and farm in partnership with Community Health Hospital South.

For three weeks this May, instead of working on this essay, I built a garden at University of Indianapolis with students in my course. We met three days a week and spent half of our time turning two vacant lots into three large garden beds by moving two large dump truck loads of soil and compost into rows, forming foot-wide walkways between rows, and planting two of the three beds. The project was a shared experience, both public and social. But there is also an element of the unknown: we know what we planted, but we don't know what it will do in new soil. The soil's pH is alkaline in the low eights, terrible for garden plants. A family of groundhogs lives under the shed next door, and, as far as they're concerned, we just planted a buffet.

This first year or two will be a fight against the soil, weather, and varmints. We'll talk with the neighbors and find ways to make the garden theirs, too. I don't know exactly what will happen, but I am fairly certain someone will do donuts in the beds with their car or truck, which we will repair. Then we will build a fence. At some point, in three or four years, it will achieve a sort of balance and stability, where we understand all of its variables and know what to plant where, a knowledge of this place closer to my grandma's knowledge of hers.

Like all gardeners—and artists—I have some vague vision of perfection. But mostly, there's nothing better than deciding what to plant and then planting it, nothing more fulfilling than harvesting a fresh purple bean or eating cherry tomatoes right off the vine—the closest way to taste the sun, something approaching tranquility.

MAMA'S BACK PORCH ON DORMAN ST.

IZERA McAFEE

The backyard mulberry bushes overflowed and bowed from fresh dew and untended years. Honeysuckle petal pieces drifted by the clothes swaying in the hot Indiana breeze, creating a humid, sweet odor. Women's white uniforms on the clothes line marked a house where a certain married woman lived—one who was spoiling a good American life for everyone else by working instead of solely caring for her children. Under the peach tree, a half-hidden stone path led to places with doors long nailed shut to accommodate today.

From the alley, a couple of scraggly bearded men searched for the porch to rest before they fell, breaking the residue of memories of dignity. They yearned for mama's homemade biscuits with strong coffee to ease embedded, though long forgotten, pain. Straight backs made an attempt to surface, to feign freedom from years of outcast logic from children clutching their mother's hands and mothers clutching their pearls. Dad checked for images of his own life in the lines on their faces to shield himself from harm. Their pale color gave rise to pride for helping someone whom others listed as the giver.

My place was being unseen in the doorway with the odd, crooked door that didn't latch right. My place was always between two worlds, and neither fit well in childhood nor beyond. Or is that the fit? Is it to stand in uncertainty about the unknown juxtaposed against temporary safety? What happens when truth sits silently on the porch?

WALKING TO THE CIRCLE: 25 MILES THROUGH A DIVIDED CITY

MICHAEL McCOLLY

Last summer, I was sitting in what was my old bedroom, staring out the window, distracted from what I was writing by a man with a briefcase walking down 71st Street. I watched him stop to let cars go by and then continue on his way to the bus stop. Every day, morning and evening, I saw him, as well as teenagers with basketballs, a young Black woman with a Kroger t-shirt, and other young people no doubt also heading to work or school along a road never designed for human beings who might want or need to walk along it. When I last lived here in my teens in the late '70s, only those with a flat tire or people peddling the Lord or poor souls with dementia would you find walking on 71st Street.

But since I moved back to Indy to help my sisters care for my mother, everywhere I go—now, of course in a car—I see people making paths on the side of the road or walking in the streets: young, old, Black, white, women with strollers, Hispanic guys on bikes.

So, the next time I saw this guy walking by my parents' home, I got off my bike to talk to him. "I walk as much as I can," he told me. "Everywhere I've lived I've walked, New York, Miami, and now Indianapolis. It's how I deal with stress of my job." But isn't that dangerous? He rolled his eyes. "I've been hit more than once—in Miami, and once here." Last year he'd been hospitalized and pointed to his leg. "The police can't do anything, they say, because, like the guy who hit me, they never stop."

Then this spring, I didn't see him anymore. But what I did see were city workers and engineers building something for the long-term health of me and my neighbors and the citizens of this city: a six-foot-wide, two-mile-long path along 71st to Binford Ave. And so, when it was completed I decided to christen it, by exploring on foot a city I never really knew nor ever believed I'd once again call home.

Leaving Home

I began on the day of the lunar eclipse, thinking that I could use whatever pull the planetary forces could provide to make my pilgrimage to Monument Circle and back before nightfall. I knew that now with the new 71st St. trail I could essentially walk almost to the Circle on one continuous trail thanks to the city's master plan to connect its greenways both through and eventually around the city. But on my return, I would zigzag along streets in neighborhoods that suffer from years of neglect and account for most of the city's alarming number of pedestrian fatalities, 82 in fact, from 2010 to 2014.

By eight-thirty I finally made it out the door and onto the trail, crossing 71st and heading west, stopping only once before Shadeland, noticing two rows of doves sunning themselves on the electrical wires running over a church parking lot—a good omen.

Walking under I-465, I had to pause just to be reminded of just how close I live to this rumbling monster that rings this city, spinning in some stretches upwards to 200,000 vehicles per day including tens of thousands of trucks.

Turning at Johnson Road, I walked along tidy sidewalks through Avalon Hills to reach Skiles Test Nature Preserve, a corner of wildness along 465 with a real dirt trail that winds down through woodlands and a meadow of goldenrod into Fall Creek gorge. In a car, you don't notice much the variation in topography, but walking you can imagine how Fall Creek was formed, sculpting out this valley as ice melt surged, tunneling under the receding glaciers carrying rock and soil with it.

A trail links the nature preserve to the Fall Creek Greenway, and through the trees, I saw a statuesque blue heron doing its best impression of a log sticking up out of a shadowy swamp. An African American couple passed in serious conversation as they got in their morning exercise, though like almost everyone I met until the Monon, they made sure they caught my eyes to greet me.

To the east, the Greenway now extends into Fort Harrison State Park, where I've come so often in the past few years, walking alone or with my mother, before she no longer could walk. But today I was heading west and strolled under the large old cottonwoods crawling with the annoying but brilliant scarlet poison ivy vines. Dads in their overly stretched spandex buzzed by on their bikes, kindly if not a bit too loudly reminding me not only that they are "on my left" but also that they are clearly of another tribe of trail user. There's tension here between walkers and cyclists as everywhere on urban trails. But except for those who believe they're in training for the Tour de France, most cyclists seemed aware that these trails are for all—wheelchair users, mothers with strollers, dog walkers, and the growing legions of baby-boomers. And this is one of the reasons why urban trails are so valuable, as they can remind us of the democratic spirit of cities Whitman sang about in his poem "Song of the Open Road:" "You road I enter upon and look around, I believe you are not all that is here, / I believe that much unseen is also here. // Here the profound lesson of reception, nor preference nor denial…"

In my younger days, the route along Fall Creek up to 56th St. was pretty much a wild area with marshes that flooded in spring where you could see thousands of birds, but it was disparaged as a place that "gays" and dope-smoking teens hung out, as well as those diehard dudes who didn't give a shit about anything except for drinking a few beers and catching catfish. So, it was somewhat ironic to see that now there's an enclave with an artificial body of water—called Lake Charlevoix. Forgive me, but if you're going to erase a wetland crucial to the health of a river basin and the wildlife it supports, could you at least give it a name that bears some respect to the actual natural history that it replaced?

Obviously, my crankiness was a sign that I needed to get to my first planned stop—my father's favorite diner, Lincoln Pancake House off Emerson. But I could see a line at the door, so I settled for a croissant and double espresso at a Starbucks, and without even stopping was marching on through Wal-Mart's parking lot and around their little retention pond where a Hispanic family was setting up for a morning of fishing.

Under Emerson Ave., I passed a party of middle-aged cyclists, smiling broadly, as their tires crackled over the fat sycamore leaves. Here I found the City Parks Department restoring a strip of land along the trail giving native wildflowers room to flourish along with future oaks and cottonwoods. This not only adds to the beauty and buffers traffic, but it creates a continuous habitat for plants and animals. Rewilding cities is not just for our pleasure and health but in some cases for the very survival of species that everywhere continue to lose precious habitat to agriculture and unchecked urban sprawl.

The demographics on the trail changed somewhat as I headed toward 38th Street. Now there were more people of color—a family biking, people fishing—as well as apartments across the river and those nondescript, concrete-block buildings housing small businesses that were so much a part of my Midwestern childhood; places where something was made or repaired or sold or all three.

At 38th Street, the river becomes off-limits and purposely disappears. This stretch is the outlet for stormwater overflow from the city's sewers, which compromises the health of this part of the river during heavy rains. Not surprisingly, this is also one of the poorer areas of the city and, as I discovered, one of the most dangerous for pedestrians.

Back in August, I spent an afternoon with an assessment team, comprised of the U.S. Dept. of Justice, the police and Public Health Departments and the YMCA, in an effort to study and develop a plan for the city to address pedestrian safety in parts of the city that suffer not only from a whole host of health problems from gun violence to inadequate sources of healthy and affordable food but also from pedestrian traffic accidents. The assessments are part of a tool designed by the Indy-based non-profit Health By Design. HBD works with cities and community organizations across the state to create safer neighborhoods and public spaces by advocating for better land use and transportation infrastructure to encourage physical activity and healthier lifestyles. Health By Design along with their partners discovered through studying police records that Marion County from 2010 to 2014 had 82 deaths attributed to auto accidents with pedestrians. And one of the locations of concern was right here on 38th Street.

I crossed over a railroad track and then the river, looking back down treeless 38th Street before finding my way back to the serene shade of the greenway, where I could see the red bridge, announcing that I'd made it to the Monon.

The traffic now is almost all bikers though there are a few runners and fewer exercise walkers (but almost no dogs). The Monon is the most well-traveled trail in the city, and one of the longest in the country. What can I say? It has changed the city—but to attract young people to this city, it's not nearly enough. The numbers of commuters are well below the average of other big cities. I'm partial to the sections that move through abandoned factories and what's left of Indy's old industrial areas and the efforts to repurpose buildings and enhance some of these neighborhoods. And I found myself marveling and completely alone under the massive sculptures of concrete and hope someday they will be just that with decades of unofficial art left from this age of the auto. But I probably won't be around to see it.

A few more hundred yards next to the thunderous traffic and I finally reached 10th Street and the city's celebrated Cultural Trail.

After a few blocks down Mass Ave following the inlaid brickwork, sleek aluminum amenities, artworks, and reminders of the generosity of the

Glick family, I got lost somewhere as the trail disappeared between buildings, but there were Marilyn and Gene, so I knew where I was. Like the Monon, kudos to the city for creating another means to encourage walking and sew together the city's cultural institutions, IUPUI, and the blooming neighborhoods around its core.

Ceremoniously I walked around the Monument Circle, noting the buffaloes with water coming from their mouths and the black bears holding up the fountains, not to mention the awkward historical boast chiseled in pure Indiana limestone of how my Hoosier ancestors "Conquered the Indians." I can't help it but every time I think about this monument, I think of that page in *Breakfast of Champions* that has left the literary world with one of the funniest images given to us by the city's most famous author that's not James Whitcomb Riley.

What I needed now was some serious food—with no option to drink alcohol, as I knew that after one microbrew I'd have to call someone to pick me up. The City Bistro let me sit outside and cool my feet off with their hose while I ate and stared at my map.

Turning back, I met a couple walking their dog and they were among the new generation who'd made the move to downtown. Semi-retired, they told me they walked everywhere and raved about what these trails have meant to them and the city.

It Gets Dangerous

Up 10th Street, back under 1-70, and the second half of my walk began. I'd planned to take another trail—Pogue's Run, a trail that when it's finished will link parts of this East Side neighborhood with the downtown. I tried to follow it as best as I could with my map but after shadowing the repurposed warehouses I cut back across the street to explore the actual namesake of the trail—Pogue's Creek, where I spied some mallards playing around in the water and decided to jump down and walk around. What a beautiful little wild place in the middle of a city.

The creek extends into Brookside Park, so I walked in this neighborhood in the rain, admiring an old stone bridge but quite aware that I was entering a part of the city that I'd never seen. It's odd to travel by foot in places where you've lived and known in one way or another for years and discover that they are as foreign as another country. A white guy walked out of his house with a big plate of red meat. A Black guy swept his porch with a little whisk broom. Walking brings with it an intimacy that you don't experience in the rushing of life in cars. Here, people's lives seemed somehow more exposed and more real. Many of the houses, though left in disrepair or abandoned, reminded me of the homes of my childhood and of the houses of my aunts and uncles and grandparents, who lived and worked in the factories and stores and shops of another Indiana that has been erased. And I felt somewhat emotional in a way I didn't expect.

Then, cutting over on Rural Street, I was about to walk under a rusted viaduct when my eye spotted what looked like old tires painted pink, several of them on a small grassy slope with flag poles and a large ribbon made of bricks painted—of course—pink, too. A shrine to breast cancer! Across the street, someone flew pink flags on a clothesline as well with more pink tires. I had to find out what this was and walked up to a Black woman getting out of her car, who told me her neighbors had done it and she'd helped them as a way to remember her mother.

After that, I felt as if I'd found the shrine of my pilgrimage and walked on down Mass Ave—but not the Mass Ave that everybody talks about. Across the railroad, I scanned the open space left from the bygone era of Indy's industrial past. Here and there, abandoned warehouses and lonely businesses stood in contrast against fields of goldenrod and weeds with stands of cottonwood returning the land to its wilder past. I walked up Roosevelt on a dirt path under electrical wires and old brick establishments, turned again and passed under 1-70, through a concrete cave, littered with debris with nests of old clothes no doubt used for makeshift beds by the homeless.

Then I cut down 25th with its array of small churches, barbershops and hair salons, and even more abandoned homes and sidewalks in disrepair. 25th ends at Sherman Ave where there is a strip mall and one of the few grocery stores in the area. I crossed at the light and unconsciously turned north not thinking that traffic from 25th could just drive on into the parking lot, and sure enough one did, as I pulled back just before being hit. How easily accidents can happen in these areas where little thought has gone into the nature of how a street is really used. Walking on down Sherman, a street with narrow sidewalks flush to the curb where four lanes of traffic rush by, I could see why it was another danger zone for pedestrians.

For several blocks, I followed a man walking ahead of me. When he turned on 32nd, I caught up with him. He had a small pack and was coming from work. His name was James Harris. He told me he walked all the time, as he didn't like to wait for the bus. When I asked about safety, he shrugged. "You have to be careful all the time, especially in winter, the snow and ice, it's not good. Better to use the bus."

When you walk all day on city streets, your perception slowly changes, and what before were just trees or cars or old buildings now become defined and take on a life and history that you would have never noticed. And though I could see the neglect of these neighborhoods and the economic struggle of its residents, I saw home-made signage, arrangements of eclectic collections of pots and plants, gardens all on display—perhaps meant for those like me who might walk by. Along Sherman, I saw an exquisitely restored Chevy Impala painted apple green cruise by with its own mellow soundtrack and pull into Raybob's Tire Shop where immediately several guys came out to admire it. Just like the murals along the Monon, I was reminded that what makes cities vibrant is not necessarily the architecture of the grand buildings and homes of the wealthy, but the individual responses of people crafted out of what they have in the places where they live.

Back on 38th Street, I'd forgotten that it was once a grand boulevard with homes set back off this street once lined with maples and oaks. And yet, going by churches and homes turned into childcare facilities, there were no sidewalks that linked bus stops, so I followed in the footsteps of others who'd made pathways before me, wondering how people managed, older people who no doubt used buses to go to church in the winter.

At last, I reached Emerson, crossed with care as the pedestrian light wasn't working, wary of those who make their quick turns oblivious to pedestrians, and walked into the grass and sat down next to a CVS parking lot. For several minutes I just sat there, cross-legged, in something of a trance, as I watched the stream of traffic and looked out over the fried food joints and the gas stations into the tops of the trees and the sky over the city. It's as if I'd traveled as another creature the last few hours, and I felt like I'd been in a river and finally been beached by the twirling eddies and will of this geography. The city was once just trees, I thought, a forest with two rivers coming together, empty of humans. And I had this thought: it's not humans who hold history, it's the land.

I'd seen trash of course all day. You walk, you see trash. You notice patterns, products, and the odd scraps and lost fragments of lives—a birthday card from a dad to a son, music lyrics from a CD, balloons and kites in trees, a metal keypunch, paperbacks, keys, playing cards, photos. Everything we have will almost all one day be trash.

Along Emerson, sidewalks were missing, or only on one side of this busy road, making people go from side to side. As Emerson winds down into the Fall Creek Valley, there are no sidewalks at all, and it's quite dangerous as there are steep drainage ditches on each side. I looked, looked again both ways, and began to trot across, just as a car came up the hill. A split second, and I'd have become one of the stats of Indy's precarious streets.

I was tired and now somewhat angry. Behind me, three adults were in a driveway talking and I turned to them and caught the African American homeowner's eye: "Hey, you guys need sidewalks out here! I almost got hit!"

"Tell me about it!" he yelled back. "You got a petition, I'll sign it!"

I felt like each time I stopped to talk with someone I was propelled into the next conversation, the trail linking me from the grad student downtown who cited studies on Indy's trails to the Black woman choking up about her mother with breast cancer to the guy walking home from work to this last young couple that I met on Fall Creek Trail. Fit and healthy, they told me they drove here two or three times a week. It was their thing to do, the young woman told me. "But why here?" I asked. Her partner, tall and lanky, leaned his head toward the river, making me look up into the sycamores one more time, "because of this."

Almost exactly 12 hours after I'd began my pilgrimage, I walked back up my parent's drive, found a beer in the fridge, and finally sat down at their kitchen table where I didn't get up for a very, very long time.

ICONS FROM INDIANAPOLIS

RUTH STONE

The fountain around the soldiers' and sailors' monument,
the mist from the splashing water, the Murat Theater;
it was there I waited for the young man I loved,
hour after hour. Often he would not come.
I leaned against the walls of a candy shop,
boxes of rubber chocolates in the window,
behind me buses snoring their pneumatic doors.
His thin bent-down body too tall
like the priest he went away to be but never was;
often exhausting even my compulsion to wait for him.
Once when he kissed me I swooned. His name was Mike Tarpey.
Even after I was engaged to someone else,
I would meet him in the park. I was not Irish. I would walk
past Our Lady of Lourdes, the sisters starched into archways
beyond the cement Pietà. I doubted even the Presbyterians.
I could see the older Black woman in the bus station,
pus running down her legs, gushing out of her,
the policeman coming to take her away. What were hats
and fur shawls when I knew that? She never left me.
From that time I carried her like an icon.
In these catacombs also he lies in perfect condition;
age nineteen, black hair, his thin jaw slightly out of line.
Was it that Picasso-like shift in planes that I could never
look at enough? These go with me where I go.
I wrap them in linens without prayers. I carry them.

MISS VICTORY (1895)

KAREN KOVACIK

Monument Circle, Indianapolis

You can't fool us, Miss Victory, queening it
over the roofs of this city, one hip swishing
toward the long sword you cock
like a walking-stick between your calves.

Girlfriend, who welded that eagle to your scalp
and posed you with the liberty torch
like some bridesmaid's lucky catch?
Why you're a certified virgin of war.

Your waist isn't wasp, there's no rumble-seat
festooning your behind. In the lingo of the parlor,
not the brawl, you remind us how we pussywhipped
the South. Are you trying to start something?

Your pectorals are rippling through your dress
and you've squared your Julius Caesar jaw.
To those shoppers down below
you're just a mannequin of camp.

No blood stipples your bronze bodice,
the polished cones of your breasts. Truth is,
you make war a costume drama, a tease,
your left hand flaming, the other hugging the hilt.

MONUMENT CIRCLE

ELIZABETH KRAJECK

Virginia Avenue to the hub,
the bus stops near Monument Circle,
we hear the driver tell of an 1820s
plan to plot the city
as if it were a wheel—
spokes are streets,
the rim, vacant land.

Joining a crowd, we walk
to the Fieldhouse for the tip-off.
When the referee throws the opening
jump ball, we lift our arms and tip
the ball to the clouds. We are the hub,
hard working, turning the wheel.

We follow the ball,
see the constellations,
spot the planets and satellites.
In the fourth quarter, we rise up for a win
for a 2-point inspiration,
a bargain for neighborhood

boys from small houses on the rim.
Champions or not we know the score,
count the necessary coins
to ride the wheel, the spokes,
a diagonal road home.
The door on the bus opens outward on earth.

The map tells us, *You are Here.*
An arrow points to the same red dot
for all of us. We understand:

Eternity runs through streets and fountains.
Restoration is half muscle, half map.
Awake all night, monuments keep score.

SOLDIERS AND SAILORS MONUMENT, INDIANAPOLIS

DAN GROSSMAN

Indiana Comic Con was last weekend.
Black Panther and N'Jadaka
are nowhere to be seen on Monument Circle

as I sit down on the steps in the afternoon light.
Across the street, WIBC is interviewing Mike Pompeo
"These are the values set by our founders,"

he says. His voice, streaming through my smartphone,
mingles with the sound of falling water
while couples walk hand in hand by the fountain

and a man takes a photo of the Statue of Victory,
of the sword grasped in her right fist.
The sculptures of another time cast their shadows over the Circle;

the charging soldiers, the home-front women
and the Black slave with chains now broken.
It's called the Civil War as if it's politely in the past

as if 400 years of history could be trumped
by the angels of our better nature.
There are no angels of our better nature.

DOWNTOWN, ANYWHERE

MALACHI CARTER

is my father
"Always watch where you're going"
"Always watch what others are doing"
"Never look at them directly"
I always looked down when I walked growing up
I remember the first time I looked up
at Monument Circle
"Is that the Statue of Liberty?"
my boyish schema asked my dad
"No, it is the Statue of Victory"
his journey from Brooklyn to Indianapolis replied
What's the difference:
liberty, victory,
book, sword,
crown, eagle's nest,
torch?

For twenty-seven years I was convinced
The Statue of Victory faced north
and had skin like mine
until I took a picture
in the tallest building
Salesforce Tower
formerly
Chase Tower
formerly
Bank One Tower
formerly
American Fletcher Tower
Fletcher Avenue
Fletcher Place (probably some white guy's name)
all
above Lady Victory
facing south

This is the closest I've ever been
to this bronze-skinned sistah
and I don't even know her actual name
only the one she was given

With a mobile camera I follow her
down her maker's assembly of history's stone still shots
come to life in my tilting and panning
surveying and strolling and shooting
Police cars on S Meridian (another European term)
I thought were corresponding to the traffic cones directing the opposite
lane
I dare
not open the doors in front of signs that say "Welcome"
In front of the cops
as they cuff escort a brotha to the back
of a paddy wagon
I didn't see them lift him
I only heard the first door shut behind me
I turned to see his last sense of freedom
There was a white wall and black holes
like a crate
My last name means one who "transports goods by cart"
a family name
my family name
mine
my father's
father's
father's
owner's
family name
my slave name

WILD IN INDIANAPOLIS

LYLANNE MUSSELMAN

Coyotes roam our city.
I'm not speaking of gangs,

packs of youths, wild and
nocturnal, who mark territory:

spray walls and tag boxcars
graffiti coloring our lives.

I'm speaking of the tricksters
that wear fur, travel on four legs,

in search of a place to call home
in our neighborhoods, to live

off the land where their ancestors
once roamed until railroads and

breakneck highways drove them out
into the rural until it grew more concrete.

Now they're back, packing like tourists
in our yards, parks, the nearest empty mall.

IN SIGHT IT MUST BE RIGHT

MICHAEL MARTONE

When you were in college, at Butler, you would drive out Michigan Pike to eat at the Steak 'n Shake there. It looked like a Steak 'n Shake but it wasn't quite right. It looked the same as other Steak 'n Shakes—black and white with the chromium fixtures and the enameled tiled walls and ceramic tile floor. The staff wore the paper hats and the check pants, the white aprons and the red bow ties. But often you were the only customer. You sat at a table, not the counter, and scanned the menu as as many as a dozen waiters and waitresses waited for you to order. This was a training restaurant for the restaurant chain, self-conscious of its self-consciousness, a hamburger university. There were waiters and waitresses in training watching how your waiter would take your order and there were waiter and waitress trainers who were being followed by other waiters and waitresses in training watching the waiter and the waiters and waitresses watching the waiter taking your order after bringing several glasses of welcoming water. They crowded around the table in their spotless uniforms like hospital interns around your bed waiting, taking notes on their checkered clipboards. There were television cameras everywhere and television monitors everywhere displaying what the television cameras were recording. There, the grill and the dozen or so trainee grill cooks pressed with the fork and spatula the meat puck into a perfect steak burger. There, one after the other flipped each patty once, crossed the instruments at right angles and pressed down again forming the perfect circles of meat, the evidence of this broadcast on snowy monitors next to those displaying the scoops of ice cream falling perfectly and endlessly into a parade of mixing shake mixing cans. There was even a monitor that showed the bank of monitors and one that showed the monitor showing that monitor and, in it the endless regression of televisions within televisions, the black-and-white-clad waiters and waitresses and the grill cooks and prep chefs moving like a chorus line, constructing your two doubles that you had ordered an acceptable duration of time ago. And the caterpillar of service snaked with your plates of perfectly plated food held by the waiter at the head-end trailed by a conga line of identical servers back to your perfect table where the television cameras panned to focus on you eating your two doubles and showing you eating your two doubles in the monitor that showed the monitor of the double you eating. And everyone in the place made sure you had everything you needed and said they'd be back to check and then came back to check and asked you if you wouldn't mind filling out the survey about the service and food and a survey about the survey and the survey about the survey's survey. The sandwiches were perfect. And the milkshake. The French fries were all exactly the same length and arranged in a pleasing random jumble. The real stainless steel cutlery gleamed and the real dishes and the glass glasses gleamed. As you left, at every empty table, an employee wiped and polished the Formica tabletop, watched over by two or three others, nodding unconsciously in what you took to be approval.

JAZZ KITCHEN

NICK READING

This kid finishes his first night
of washing dishes and steak knives
when he hangs the apron and walks
into a room with short ceilings and long,

very long legs. He comes up to
their waists. His image of the blues
pales in this gray. Cigarettes are tongues
flicked and ashed over. Louise Misha,

he will remember that name, leans
into a moan. A yellow shower of dust
settles in her hair. The piano slinks.
This kid, unsure as most, drinks

too much. At this moment he could fall
in love. He might decide to be late for
the rest of his life. As if he will never
want to leave the Kitchen as he considers

the dark stalls in the bathroom, his face
sore from its serious contortions.
Remember that jazz? Time had no name.
Suffering had no register.

FLORAL LADY'S EMPLOYER FILES FOR BANKRUPTCY

NATALIE SOLMER

The newspapers say we're dying, say retail apocalypse.
I am thinking I have saved the lives of many sad ferns.

We've been patiently waiting for this since Mr. Marsh's troubles (women, drink and
    airplanes)
and subsequent buy out. But let it be known he paid us better, and let it be known

for thirteen years I have poured cup after cup
teaspoon after teaspoon of water, fertilizer,

into orchids, for instance until the buds have broken open
in this cold hemisphere, hallelujah, my mind still rich in poverty.

Actually I have seen my own blood obsessed with nothing but choosing tile
and comparing their things with the neighbors' things. They don't believe me

punching in and out on the timeclock every week. It's a horror to them
that full time, and I still need, accept welfare. They get out calculators.

The cool thing is that they can't even see me. They are doing very important things
when they go on vacation. My life has revolved around a series of leaky sinks.

I have done the things I was terrified of—touched dripping packages of meat,
held and counted the soft currency of strangers, made 200 prom corsages in a day,

ordered the lilies, etc. with an electronic gun and procured them from the dairy
    cooler
and hauled the pallets and cut bunches and moved and arranged and dealt

with the angry women wanting freshest alstroemeria from the back. I've also been
just some girl stacking shopping carts into the corral or watering the stacks of mums
    outside.

I am not leaving until they close all doors. I have stood on my own two tennis-shoed
    feet,
trying not to soak them with the garden hose, the watering can, the glass vases,

my slapdash wild arrangements—fuchsias and oranges and yellows and there are
    some blues
you can use or create from a can of paint. I have created my world in my corner

by the bread aisle and salad bar that's never as cold as it should be, no matter
which one of the nine stores I worked in when 'floating' and fluffing up a mess.

I have wiped down the black counters and white floors of the universe each sunset.
I have ducked my head into hidden books, notebooks, and hurried my hands for this
    quiet

after each year's cut back after cut back until this bankrupt summer I wait with the
    others
who wait. We want to watch the destruction close-up, but still need a roof over our
    heads,

our rent checks. What do you think of us? I have used all these plants that use their
    blooms
for their sexy advertisements. I have delivered these poesies to alter the air

around both the newly dead and the newly born. I have turned face after face of
    sunflower,
daisy, carnation, and rose to meet the ravenous day, and with its people, I will wait.

REQUIEM OF A WOMANIST LIBRARY TRUSTEE

DR. TERRI JETT

Everyone has a library story. Many families have done as I did when I first moved to a new place—my children and I went downtown to the Indianapolis public library. I remember it was large, seemed a little dark, but there was an elaborate children's section, down a wide set of stairs. It was also conveniently the location for the only public restrooms in the library at that time, according to my friend Jim Roundtree who retired from there after 37 years of service—so he should know. He said it was also a hot spot for drag queens, so our current Drag Queen Story Hour seems an appropriate way to celebrate their history. Like them I saw the public library as a safe place, welcoming to all regardless of who you are or how you are perceived. As a child growing up in Richmond, California I spent many hours at the public library because it was right next door to my father's office located in City Hall. If you were a regular, the librarians there would have suggested books waiting for you that were usually spot on.

It was not until I was appointed to the Indianapolis Public Library (IndyPL) Board of Trustees did I consider the operations of the library and the complexities of the public face vs. private face. When teaching students about critical feminist theory there is an emphasis on how the second wave feminist movement led to the foreground issues women face in the private sphere that require a public response—such as the value of traditional roles of women in their households, the responsibilities of motherhood and childcare that disproportionately alter the trajectory of the careers of women. And then there is the private issue of domestic violence, which requires a public response situated in the justice system which to date, has been woefully unprepared to address it. The current COVID-19 pandemic, and the state-sanctioned "shelter-at-home" policy response neglected to consider the unintended danger that has subsequently led to an increase in domestic violence here and throughout the world. And where the public library may provide some tools for addressing these struggles, the feminist lens recognizes that as an institution it has its own private-facing challenges that leave it ill-equipped to serve as a panacea to all that ails the public.

My introduction to my position as a library trustee was met with microaggressions cast in an "orientation" process that was proceeded with an essay sent to me by the then president of the Board at the time titled, "Stay in Your Lane" with a follow-up meeting where it was "revealed" that there was knowledge of me being a "friend" of the library union president—as if this is something I was trying to hide and had suddenly been exposed as a spy. Just scratching the surface one would find that I'm the daughter of a retired post office worker and public accountant and a retired member of the California Nurses Association who has often participated in the efforts of Jobs With Justice (JWJ) and Unite Here! The JWJ Scrooge Party is one of my favorite holiday events. And sending an essay to any Black person about staying in one's lane is a throwback to fifties era segregation rhetoric that with a generous reading had the mark of subconscious color blindness. I was just thankful that the combination of my lived experience, my degree in Ethnic Studies, and the fact that I went to graduate school in Alabama (solid training ground) and my intuition as a Sagittarius (yes, that matters) moved me to grab my Black womanist intellectual armor and prepare for battle. My favorite author, Alice Walker first introduced the term womanist in her 1979 collection of essays, *In Search of Our Mothers' Gardens*, where she uses the term to describe the intersectional experiences of Black feminist women.

I have read and heard about the notion of armor from many women of color that find themselves in unwelcome arenas that would otherwise be ripe for their visioning if they would just assimilate and prop up the status quo. And some do to save themselves from the exhaustion of fighting against their presumed incompetence, the constant questioning of their knowledge, and the disregard of their perspectives. And yet the clarity of the institutional public/private divide cannot be ignored because any study of organizational and societal transformation understands that the mechanism for accountability and redress do not often exist within the framework of the institution itself or even in the system where that institution is located, in this case, the public system, an awkward predicament. Therefore, the ability to affect real change, even when one is situated in proximity to power often requires the marginalized individual to give voice to their own truth, a risky endeavor.

The last thing someone should tell me is to "stay-in your-lane." Just the mere suggestion is going to move me to do quite the opposite. The "orientation" essay was actually about the proper role of the Board in relation to the Administration, which reports to the Board; but that is nothing new and at certain points could be a necessary conversation. But that title is never appropriate, aside from the fact that it is an overused cliché. And the ever-present wisdom of my father rang in my ear in the form of a Kenny Rogers song, "Know when to hold 'em, know when to fold 'em, know when to walk away, and know when to run." I was sittin' at the table with players who felt they held a royal flush.

In the notes of a Library Board retreat, which I did not attend because I place a high value on how my time is spent, there was common agreement reached that the private space of disagreements should not be aired in the public of social media or when the camera is rolling because, after all, that would be uncivil. Those present included the then-president of the Board, who served on the City Council with the Library's CEO, a newly elected city councilor, a fairly recently appointed to the Board elected judge and a Baptist minister the VP of the Board who said to me during my orientation process, "You sure ask a lot of questions." By the time of that retreat, I knew that three people were leaving the Board including the then-president, who had joined the Board at least a year after I did, had missed several meetings and chaired no committees. And while I did not know the new appointees, I engaged in an institutional process primarily for the gift of revelation. I ran for president of the Board and lost by a vote of four-three. Four men against the three Black women on the Board. I came prepared to the Board meeting with a statement of my dedication and involvement for the three years to date that I had served including chairing two committees, attending many programs and events including staff day and two Indiana Library Federation conferences and serving as a liaison to the Indianapolis Public Library Foundation. The board member running against me had served for less than a year, chaired no committees but mentioned that he frequented one of the branches with his son. There seems to be a pattern in how one becomes the president of the Library Board.

The VP running that particular meeting of the election said that I should've mentioned to him prior to the Board meeting that I would come with a prepared statement and that he had to consult with the Board attorney as to whether or not I would be "allowed" to read my statement. After all, he suggested, it was unfair that I was prepared and the judge (a seasoned political official) running against me was not. "Come on, Dr. Jett, you know better." I haven't heard that phrase since I was ten, only echoed by the language of "disappointment," that many women often hear in the workplace from their male supervisors. A previous Library Board member gave me sound advice when he said, "You win when you learn how to count to four." Got it—One potato, two potato....

The public face of a library that serves a county of roughly a million people is multi-layered and highly political. It carries the weight of trying to provide something for everyone with very limited financial resources in comparison to other neighboring county libraries who serve fewer but have a wealthier tax base to draw from and only one facility versus twenty-four. In fact, for IndyPL there is a relatively clear distinction between the use of public funds for operational and capital development purposes and the gift of private funding for programming which comes through the Indianapolis Public Library Foundation. I had no idea until I became a Library Board trustee that the foundation even existed; after all, I had been to many programs of the library but I didn't recall ever being asked for a contribution. I discovered from my high-level perch—which afforded me a fairly brief stint as a liaison to the foundation—that like many philanthropic organizations there is a disregard for working-class people like me who are not asked to contribute to something where we could also be beneficiaries. And why would this savior complex be disrupted when a) it has proud roots; b) it works for the most part and c) it does not disrupt the decision-making process in place of the institutional beneficiary. "It is important to remember that we are a SEPARATE organization," I was told as part of my library foundation orientation. So noted.

The library programs are most often the brainchild of library staff who fight through the bureaucratic fog with an eye towards the realities of what is before them and the limitations imposed on possibilities. For some of them it is their responsibility to come up with programs and for them and the rest of the staff it is simply their passion for public service that drives them. The public sees an abundance of free programs and services but the private-facing structure is shaped by an inadequate reward system wrought with confusion and inequities and cast in a false system of meritocracy that is oddly governed by a strategic plan that some staff finds only vaguely recognizable to their daily activities. I bore witness to the challenges of programming when I agreed to serve as a moderator in a series of community discussions centering around what would have been the 90th year birthday of Reverend Dr. Martin Luther King, Jr. The amazing librarian that submitted the request for funding, for cookies, water, and a little publicity, had to wait for months to find out whether or not her program would receive funding. This was one time where I thought the participation of a board member might help but then I remembered "my place." The process at the time was something like: proposals submitted across the system only one time around March for the following fiscal year and decisions made at some point around November or December. Our program began in January which meant the hustle was on once we were notified with the go-ahead. It seems a rolling submission process might work better—but what do I know—I'm just a Board member and suggestions from me are usually met initially with pause, circular conversation, and no results. "The parking lot at the new library branch seems too small," I offered at a Board meeting. Pause, rejection, and then months later an expansion of the parking lot at the new branch. Sometimes, I'm wrong...

A few of the libraries are within walking distance to public high schools where a number of the students, especially those without after-school-sanctioned extracurricular activities on certain days will head to the public library for what I'm assuming are a number of reasons—such as to study, maybe just to hang out, or perhaps it serves as a safe place. I don't really know because I haven't asked them and nor has anyone else connected to the library. I could be wrong, but I haven't seen any evidence to the contrary. It really is a simple question, "Why are you coming here after school?" Phrased differently it could also be stated, "Thank you for coming, do you have everything you need from us as far as materials and services?" Instead what I was presented with as a Board member is a "problem," necessitating a $400,000 increase in security that I took personally considering that one of those libraries was often frequented after school by my daughter. For months, when we used to receive a dashboard of statistics at every Board meeting, we were presented with a flatline of teen participation that was being addressed by the one enthusiastic teen specialist we met on occasion. As far as I can tell she was not a regular presence at either of the "problem" library branches and when I asked about more documentation of the problem I was told, "I don't have to give you that information." When I gave womanist voice to this response through my social media noting this as resistance to the authority of a Black woman it was deemed as uncivil, the problem of airing the dirty laundry of the private sphere in a medium that should always be assumed to be public. A new concept became a regular feature of communication— "off-line." "Dr. Jett, if you have any questions, I'm happy to address them "off-line." Translation: "In private."

The public face of the library shores up the heroic efforts of the staff, the cute pictures of kids buried in books, the introduction of a new website, and the groundbreaking of new branches, carefully designed to organically blend in with the neighborhoods they serve. The private face of the library necessitated the creation of a union to protect the frontline workers, discussions about the lack of diversity in various contractual opportunities, the need for real social workers versus the expectations of librarians to stretch their job responsibilities to serve in that capacity and the navigation of a multi-year shifting study of the appropriateness of a 360-evaluation process seen as a hostile suggestion rather than a standard practice for countless similarly-sized organizations. Situated in a public system that values transparency, the womanist library board trustee is often reminded that this same system is political and therefore its limitations are bound by the private whims of individuals rather than the collective conscious of the community it serves. So, I trudge on hanging on to my favorite Eleanor Roosevelt quote, "No one can make you feel inferior without your consent." I arm myself with the actual handbook that provides some clarity as to what my role and power is as a library board trustee in the state of Indiana and even when a fairly new member of the so-called executive team tries to school me on what I can and cannot do from his unearned high perch, I sit back and wait for the hand to be played—it's not a royal flush; after all, that's just two pair.

"MORAL WARFARE": INDIANAPOLIS WOMEN'S LONG-FOUGHT BATTLE FOR THE VOTE

NICOLE POLETIKA

Dr. Amelia Keller rushed, sweating and weary from lack of sleep, to Indianapolis's Claypool Hotel, where her like-minded sisters convened. When asked why she was late, the doctor replied that she "had just welcomed a new suffragist into the world." Obtaining suffrage—a term that, for many, conjures up images of dowdy women marching for *something-or-the-other*—would mean women could influence the laws that impacted them, from maternal health care to working conditions. In other words, they would be U.S. citizens imbued with the same rights as their husbands, pastors, and sons. One woman at the 1911 meeting asked Dr. Keller how she thought Indiana's lawmakers could be convinced to support women's right to vote. The president of the Woman's Franchise League, no doubt exasperated by the lack of progress in a movement that began in 1851, responded that the only strategy left was to "get out and collect $1,000,000 and buy" the legislature. She quipped, "Men of education and refinement can be reached by argument and reason.... They would scorn the use of money, but such men are scarce in the Indiana legislature."

The audacity and innovation of Hoosier women in their fight for the ballot box are at odds with the idea that Indiana has eternally been a conservative state. In fact, ardent Indianapolis suffragist Harriet Noble couched the movement in radical terms, stating that suffragists were "engaged in warfare—moral warfare—an assault on prejudice and ignorance." Equally surprising, considering the political polarization of the twenty-first century, were Hoosier suffragists' willingness to cross party, socioeconomic, racial, and religious lines in order to achieve their singular goal. Exploring this movement, which thrummed from Indianapolis out to every corner of the state like the spokes of a wheel, is not only inspiring but could provide a blueprint for modern-day political compromise and grassroots mobilization. There is still work to do. After all, the Equal Rights Amendment has yet to be ratified 97 years after Alice Paul introduced it in Congress.

It's easy to assume that American women's suffrage was a foregone conclusion, that in a Democratic country, things would sort themselves out. But Hoosier suffragists, enduring defeat after defeat, took to their automobiles, to the printing press, and to the halls of the statehouse in their quest for equality. Knowing that no one else would do it for them, enterprising women founded suffrage and citizenship schools to educate women on the political process. They went to factories and department stores to inform working women why they would benefit from the right to vote. They spoke at Farmers' Institutes and handed out 50,000 flyers to state fairgoers in order to reach rural women. Unwavering Indianapolis suffragist and columnist Grace Julian Clarke insisted it was women's persistence alone that led to ratification of the 19th Amendment, as they had battled "extremely uphill efforts—not one generation of them, but generation after generation, in all parts of the country."

Indiana's fight originated not in Indianapolis, but in Wayne County. Inspired by Quaker efforts towards women's equality, Dublin hosted Indiana's first woman's rights convention in 1851. Attendees adopted resolutions supporting women's political and social rights, as well as equal pay for equal work, and the following year formed the Indiana Woman's Rights Association (IWRA). Richmond's Dr. Mary Thomas became the first woman to address the state's legislature when in 1859 she petitioned for married women's property law and women's suffrage. She spoke with humility, but directness, lamenting that "Thousands of women in public positions are practically living down the old stereotyped insult to women, that restriction alone can keep her virtuous." She condemned the fact that "the law, with its ruthless hand, undertakes to 'settle her business for her,' when she had no voice in making that law." The legislature regarded the address flippantly, as they did when Indianapolis suffragist Zerelda Wallace presented a petition for prohibition signed by 10,000 women. One state senator told her they might as well be the signatures of 10,000 mice.

The Civil War soon disrupted this momentum, as women on the home front busied themselves with nursing wounded soldiers and procuring supplies for relief efforts. Dr. Anita Morgan noted in her *We Must Be Fearless: The Woman Suffrage Movement in Indiana*, that IWRA meetings resumed in 1869, the first-year historians can document the participation of African Americans in Hoosier suffrage meetings. If the disregard of legislators and a national crisis weren't enough to overcome, suffragists who had convinced the 1881 Indiana General Assembly to amend the constitution to allow for women's suffrage had to deal with the fact that amendments had to be approved by *two* legislative sessions. Curiously enough, when legislators reconvened in 1883 the law was nowhere to be found, and thus couldn't be voted on.

Perhaps this defeat is what led to a stall in the efforts of Hoosier suffragists. The renowned Susan B. Anthony attempted to jar Hoosier women awake in her December 20, 1897 letter to Indiana's patron saint of suffrage, May Wright Sewall. After working sixteen-hour days for suffrage at the national level, Anthony warned against making excuses writing, "So you young folks must not talk of hard times nor the opposition of other work, nor family cares nor anything under the sun but just to push through to the best of your ability." She begged Sewall, whom she deeply valued for her organizational skills, to "hold on, and hope on."

Anthony would probably struggle to "hope on," as Indiana's suffrage organizations essentially lay dormant. It wasn't until 1911 that Indianapolis firebrands Grace Julian Clarke and Dr. Amelia Keller put a defibrillator on the weakly beating chest of Indiana's suffrage movement. After lobbyists failed to convince the legislature to pass partial or municipal suffrage bills, the two women realized the need to overcome apathy and seriously mobilize, forming the Indiana Woman's Franchise League (WFL). In an article proclaiming, "Family Unharmed by Mother's Interest in Suffrage," Eugenie Nicholson, social reformer and wife of famous Indianapolis author Meredith Nicholson, agreed that the time was right to push for an expansion of women's rights. As technology began liberating women from the home—no longer were they forced to sew every item of their children's clothing—women increasingly worked at "business houses." In this industrializing society, it was "manifestly unfair that they should be deprived the right of a voice in governing the conditions under which they work." Mary Butler Jameson gave another reason for women's suffrage in an *Indianapolis Star* article and argued that women would do best "controlling the destinies of nations." Whereas men gave millions of dollars to war, women would give to education, and while "men engage in politics for business reasons," women would engage in politics to improve living conditions.

Through the efforts of these ardent women, the capitol city soon became a hub of suffrage parades, street meetings, and fundraising galas. Hundreds of Hoosiers dressed in their finest, among them doctors, ministers, and lawyers, rubbed elbows on the Indianapolis lawn of former U.S. vice president Charles W. Fairbanks. Some feasted on hot roasted peanuts and flipped through newly purchased literature while waiting their turn to consult with Eldena Lauter, the endlessly popular fortune-teller. With answers to life's deepest questions in tow, they might head to the dance pavilion, spinning with their partners under brightly colored bunting and strings of electric lights. Perhaps the men and women would opt to hear English suffragist and *Titanic* survivor Elsie Bowerman speak in favor of women's right to vote. Others observed the performance of an "opray," where the "musical sarcasm" of the suffragists made the few anti-suffragists in attendance laugh against their will. The evening ended with a parade, where nearly everyone sported the "suffrage sunflower" pin. The "funfest," perhaps strategically named to counter the stereotype that a suffragist was inherently a dour and "masculinely impossible female," raised funds to support the activities of the Woman's Franchise League.

From garden parties at Fletcher Sanitorium to dances (Gasp, were they a proper form of fundraising? "Suffragists can dance as well as any one," Noble quipped.), Indy's reformers grew savvy at raising awareness and money for their cause. But they also realized the need to engage in political activism in a less insular setting. Energized, the women hit the streets and sidewalks, piling into cars and motoring over to neighboring Hamilton County, where they passed out flyers to businessmen, courthouse officials, and city "loafers." The women so-engaged Noblesville locals that they abandoned a tent show production of "From Rags to Riches" in favor of discussing suffrage bills. *The Indianapolis News* remarked that "Sex equality supplanted theatricals as the topic of conversation and debate" in the city's square. The women had even more success in Westfield, where local women committed to forming a WFL branch.

The honing of their persuasive chops served Indy's suffragists well as they increasingly confronted the men who made Indiana's laws. Donning "warpaint of fine feathers and pretty gowns," and draped in yellow "Votes for Women" banners, 500 suffragists marched on the statehouse in 1913. Scorning the elevator in favor of the stairs—in a show of tenacity—they permeated the capital building like rays emanating from the sun. "Jammed in the Senate," the women demanded that the legislature amend the constitution to remove the word "male" as criteria to vote. In decades-long tradition "evasion was the game," of the legislators, despite being "buttonholed in every corner of the big chamber by women."

If anything, this legislative defeat galvanized the suffragists who, led by Clarke, formed the Woman's Legislative Council in 1914. This lobbying group, financed by ministers, businessmen's clubs, churches, and farmers' associations, held lawmakers' feet to the fire regarding bills related to women's rights. Representing 50,000 Hoosier women from groups like the

Council of Jewish Women and Women's Press Club, the women of the WLC kept their fingers on the pulse of the goings-on of Indiana's elected officials. Securing an office in the statehouse, suffragists, who included Wellesley and Vassar College graduates, worked alongside AP statehouse reporters. WLC members placed informative pamphlets on the desks of lawmakers and took detailed records on each legislator's voting records to be used for future decisions. The women were becoming as adept at bathing disobedient children as they were persuading apathetic lawmakers as to the merits of women's enfranchisement.

Suffragists continued to keep the issue in front of the public. At Fountain Square's May Day festivities, honoring Indianapolis's laborers, suffragists slipped pro-suffrage literature into the hands of reform-minded celebrants. Meanwhile, between Illinois Street and Monument Circle, a bugle sounded, summoning 300 men and women, on foot and in cars, who favored women's equality. They listened to Luella McWhirter read the Woman's Declaration of Independence and the Anthony Amendment (what would become the 19th Amendment). These, like other towns and cities across the U.S., were delivered to the president in an effort to convince him to support women's suffrage. Mr. W.D. Headrick, standing in his open-air automobile, implored those within earshot to acknowledge women as *human beings*, worthy of rights. He proclaimed, "She has a heart and a mind, and was not created a mechanical doll just to amuse men." She had a right to influence modern conditions, not by "praying on bended knee and in supplication." No, she should be able to "do it fighting, and armed with the same weapon a man has, the ballot." She too paid taxes. Where was her representation?

Being that many of Indianapolis's suffragists were white and financially well-off, WFL members recognized the need to be more representative and inclusive within the local movement. They sought new partners in the historic fight for equal rights and pledged to "come into closer contact with the great majority of women who make up the laboring classes." Noble spoke before attendees of the Central Labor Union's meeting at Washington Street. She acknowledged that the majority of suffragists belonged to the "leisure class," but that the movement needed the support of working women because they "are the ones who will be most benefited by the vote when it is granted." Fellow suffragist Anna Dunn Noland was able to secure the endorsement of 1,600 miners at a national convention in Indianapolis. These efforts proved fruitful and franchise organizations often got the backing of unions and working women, who shared an interest in guarding human rights.

Along with organized labor, suffragists sought the support of Indianapolis's African American community. Equal Suffrage Association (ESA) branch president Dr. Hannah Graham, along with African American leaders like Freeman Ransom, helped found Indianapolis's African American branch of the ESA, No. 7. None other than revered Black entrepreneur, Madame C.J. Walker, hosted the branch's first meeting at her home, where African American public-school teacher Carrie Barnes was elected president. Of the branch's work, Barnes proclaimed, "We all feel that colored women have need for the ballot that white women have, and a great many needs that they have not." Black suffragists hosted debates at the Senate Avenue YMCA and local African American churches and worked with white ESA branches and trade unions to forward women's right to vote. The unlikely collaboration of Indianapolis's privileged white women, laboring classes, and African American community would help lead to the ratification of women's suffrage.

This hopeful coalition had reason to celebrate in 1917 when the legislature enacted a partial suffrage bill. The WFL set up booths at shopping venues to inform women, perhaps stocking up on E-Z BAKE flour or Pinkham's Veggie Compound, about the importance of exercising their new right. Some Hoosier women became notaries, so they could register women to vote as they canvassed neighborhoods. But, like so many times before, the figurative ballot was plucked from their hands when the state's supreme court ruled the law unconstitutional. The women had come too far to turn back and, in the words of suffragist Marie Edwards, "The taste of power has been fatal." Women who hadn't so much as considered voting rights wanted to know why they had been taken away. Edwards looked at the glass as half-full stating, "The fact remains that for a while we were voters, and all the effect of that is not lost."

On the precipice was an event that would change the course of history and the fortunes of suffragists: World War I. While U.S. troops battled in European trenches, women mobilized to support war efforts, darning slippers for hospitalized soldiers and cultivating victory gardens. Unlike the Civil War, women's suffrage did not take a backseat to warfare, and instead, suffragists utilized the global conflict as an opportunity to demonstrate their competencies and civic worth. Historian Dr. Anita Morgan noted that "what the war managed to do was to finally focus the energies of all these suffragists and club women so they acted in concert for one goal— win the war and in the process win suffrage for themselves." Suffragists pointed out the hypocrisy of fighting for democracy while depriving American women of their rights. Red Cross workrooms and Liberty Bond drives provided forums for suffragists to inform their patriotic colleagues of the value of the vote. Through this activism, the WFL had established 238 local branches across the state and this burgeoning network continued to agitate for the vote after the conclusion of the war.

"Scenes of the wildest joy and confusion" played out at the statehouse on January 16, 1920, when legislators at a special session voted to make Indiana the 26th state to ratify the 19th Amendment to the U.S. Constitution. After a "storm of applause in the chamber," a crowd of elated women, who probably felt as if their feet hardly touched the marble steps, descended upon Governor Goodrich to offer their gratitude. A band outside the House struck up a jubilee. Suffragist Helen Benbridge praised Indiana's legislators, who had "been giving us oratory for years when we wanted action." She announced that while the nation waited for the requisite 36 states to ratify the federal amendment, the WFL would set up citizenship schools with the goal to make "every woman an intelligent voter in 1920." The WFL accomplished this by becoming a branch of the League of Women Voters. Reflecting on the momentous occasion, Benbridge pointed out that while Indianapolis played a leading role in obtaining the vote, the achievement should also be attributed to "the women over the State."

Women wearing "boudoir caps and gowns" lined Indianapolis polling stations on November 2, 1920. "Contrary to expectations," they didn't find voting machines bewildering and, in fact, *The Indianapolis News* reported, "Old-fashioned politicians, who formerly croaked their doubts about the ability of women in politics, rapidly changed their minds when they saw what the women were doing." An estimated 71,000 of Marion County's 76,000 women voted, some with children in tow and others staffing the polling booths. Precincts with Black and German populations turned out at higher rates. In exercising their civic duty, the women proved wrong anti-suffragists' arguments that husbands spoke for their wives at the polls and that families would fall apart while the women were in the voting booth. Many probably felt a sense of empowerment as they cast their vote, and certainly, those who had lobbied for suffrage had a newfound confidence in themselves and a new set of skills.

In these anxious modern times, where women's autonomy over their own bodies is continually threatened and a man accused of sexual assault was sworn in as a U.S. Supreme Court judge, the exit of Senator Elizabeth Warren from the 2020 presidential race felt like the ringing of a death knell for many Democratic women. *Medium* columnist Jessica Valenti lamented,

"It's enough to make me feel, well, despairing: that we had the candidate of a lifetime—someone with the energy, vision, and follow-through to lead the country out of our nightmarish era—and that the media and voters basically outright erased and ignored her." It was doubly painful coming on the heels of Hillary Clinton's loss in the 2016 presidential election to a man who notoriously bragged "when you're a star, they let you do it, you can do anything... grab them by the pussy."

Disheartening as this is, the women's suffrage movement should give us hope that, while it may take much, *much* longer than it should, women's equality can be achieved. The movement also taught us that it is incumbent upon women to organize and advocate for their own rights. It requires sustaining the momentum and solidarity of the women's marches that followed Donald Trump's election. Grace Julian Clarke, a "nasty woman" in her time, certainly understood the collective frustration of women, remarking, "Sometimes we sigh because members of the legislature and of Congress are not all the very wisest, most virtuous, and polished." Her strategy to influence these elected officials remains relevant, even in these contentious times. She advised, "whatever they are, we have to deal with them, to appeal not only to the best in them, but to their prejudices sometimes, to their business interests perhaps, or to family, church of social affiliation."

SARAH'S EXODUS

SHARI WAGNER

Madame C.J. Walker (Sarah Breedlove) 1867-1919
America's first female self-made millionaire

I was born in a sharecropper's shack,
with no windows and a dirt floor,
but when Mama twisted my hair
in ribbons made from rags,

I knew I was the picture
of Pharaoh's daughter
who found the baby Moses
all alone in a cotton field.

When Mama died, I missed
the tug of her fingers on my hair,
their firm resolve. My sister's
twisting was too loose. She married

a brute who beat me with his fist
and cursed my hair that fell
in clumps like I was an ugliness
not worth holding onto. I escaped

when I turned fourteen and married
a man named Moses, but the sea
that should have parted, spread
its blood-stained sheet, leaving me

a widow, nursing a child
whose crown I kissed to make it real.
In St. Louis, lye soap burned
my forearms raw, but I'd toil past

midnight, hunched over an iron tub
so Lelia could have food and schooling,
I scrubbed in that sweltering fog
till one night when the Lord

delivered a dream: an African
angel-man who anointed
my scabby scalp with "Madam
C.J. Walker's Wonderful Hair Grower."

He handed me the recipe
and I stood up. I stood up
and pulled other washerwomen
stooped over rusty tubs

into a door to door force
selling on commission. I built
my factory in Indianapolis
and swam in money I would have

sunk under if I had clutched.
But my hands were open.
I never forgot the bruised bodies
hanging beneath magnolia leaves

or the bent-over women washing
taffeta and lace with never anything
pretty for themselves. Once I dreamed
of brushing Mama's hair,

and as I brushed, her sparse hair
grew thick and curled out the door,
down the street, so that people
gasped and still I stroked,

till blackness shone like the sea
Moses parted and I began to braid.

THE STORY BEHIND TELLING MADAM C. J. WALKER'S STORY

A'LELIA BUNDLES

When *Self Made: Inspired by the Life of Madam C. J. Walker*—the Netflix series starring Oscar winner Octavia Spencer—premiered on March 20, 2020, millions of people around the world heard Madam Walker's name for the first time. Thousands of people, who already knew at least a little bit about her, tuned in with hopes of learning something new.

I could tell from the reaction on social media that there's an audience hungry for a story of Black women's empowerment and African American success. There's also a core group of Madam Walker fans who wrote elementary school reports about her and cosmetologists who followed in her footsteps. They have been waiting for decades for this particular tale. The excitement reminds me of the 1950s and 1960s when those of us of a certain age ran to our televisions on the rare occasions when a Black person appeared on *The Ed Sullivan Show* or when Nat King Cole finally hosted a show in 1956. Of course, in 2020, we have many other viewing options, but as Walker's biographer and great-great-granddaughter, I've come to know how attached many people feel and how personally they identify with anything related to Madam Walker. It's wonderful to see so much interest and anticipation.

But long before Hollywood came calling, many people recognized the power of Madam Walker's story and identified with her struggles. The seeds that were planted decades ago are in full bloom. A century after her death, Madam Walker is having a moment.

In 1955, I felt my first moment of Walker magic when I opened my grandmother's dresser drawer and found miniature mummy charms and receipts from the 1922 trip my great-grandmother, A'Lelia Walker took to Cairo. I was only three years old and had no idea that that discovery would lead me to write *The Joy Goddess of Harlem: A'Lelia Walker and the Harlem Renaissance,* a biography that will be published by Scribner in 2022.

I wrote my first report about A'Lelia Walker in 1970 when I was a senior in high school. As a student at Columbia University's Graduate School of Journalism in 1975, I was encouraged by Professor Phyl Garland to write my master's paper about Madam Walker. At the time, there still was no major biography of Madam Walker or A'Lelia Walker.

Stanley Nelson's 1989 *Two Dollars and a Dream*, was the first documentary about Madam Walker and can now be seen in its entirety on YouTube. Nelson, whose grandfather Freeman B. Ransom was general manager and general counsel for the Madam C. J. Walker Manufacturing Company, also directed and produced *BOSS: The Black Experience in Business*, a 2019 nonfiction film that includes historically accurate information about Madam Walker.

In 1982, Alex Haley, whose fame from the 1976 *Roots* miniseries still was cresting, approached us about producing a Madam Walker project. For the next several years, Alex was a helpful mentor as I traveled to more than a dozen American cities doing primary source research and interviewing nearly twenty people who had known, worked with, or been friends of Madam Walker and A'Lelia Walker.

On a freighter trip from Long Beach, California to Guayaquil, Ecuador with Alex and two other writers, I finished the manuscript for *Madam C. J. Walker: Entrepreneur,* a young adult biography published in 1991.

It's stunning to think this was the first book-length biography of Madam Walker ever published, especially now that my personal library is filled with more than 200 books that chronicle Madam Walker's life, from Tiffany Gill's *Beauty Shop Politics,* Noliwe Rooks's *Hair Raising*, and Kathy Peiss's *Hope in a Jar* to Hillary and Chelsea Clinton's *The Book of Gutsy Women,* Jean Case's *Be Fearless,* and The Undefeated's *The Fierce 44.*

And the scholarship continues. Indiana University professor Tyrone McKinley Freeman's *Madam C. J. Walker's Gospel of Giving: Black Women's Philanthropy during Jim Crow* was published in November 2020. Since the 1970s, many people have worked together on a range of initiatives to preserve Madam Walker's legacy. Among the projects: a campaign for the 1998 Madam Walker U. S. postage stamp; restoration of the Madam Walker Legacy Center in Indianapolis; designation of Villa Lewaro [Madam C. J. Walker's Estate in New York's Hudson Valley] as a National Trust for Historic Preservation National Treasure; digitization of more than 40,000 items in the Madam Walker Collection at the Indiana Historical Society where a twenty-eight-month Madam Walker exhibition—"You Are There: Madam Walker 1915"—opened in September 2019; renaming of 136th Street at the corner of Malcolm X Boulevard (Lenox Avenue) as Madam C. J. Walker and A'Lelia Walker Place in July 2019; creation of the Madam Walker Family Archives, the largest privately owned collection of Walker business records, photographs and memorabilia; dozens of Madam Walker dolls and amazing fine art like Sonya Clark's large installation at the Austin's Blanton Museum and Indianapolis's Alexander Hotel; introduction of MCJW, a new line of Madam Walker hair care products manufactured by Sundial Brands.

So, yes, the Netflix series has introduced Madam Walker to many people who otherwise would never have known about her. After you've watched the Hollywood version—where the writers have used a great deal of creative license to heighten the drama with characters who didn't exist and scenes that didn't occur in real life—we hope you will become curious enough to seek the facts.

PINK POODLE

WILL HIGGINS

The 5-foot 1-inch, 130-pound Russian-born Isaac "Tuffy" Mitchell gets no play in any telling of the story of Indianapolis, not even a footnote. Mitchell has been expunged from history.

That's strange because he was prominent. How prominent?

When Mitchell died (at age 56, Sept. 30, 1970, at 2:30 a.m., while shooting pool at the Happy Landing Tavern, 1401 E. 73rd St., of natural causes), the city's leading newspaper spared readers no detail, reporting how much cash Mitchell had in his pockets ($802) and what was in his car, a Buick (one pool cue, one 20-piece dinnerware set, two radios, four Bibles, one set of false teeth).

But today few people have even heard of Tuffy Mitchell. The man who'd insisted he was a "charitable saint" even as a judge was giving him five years for tax fraud was swept under the rug.

And his Pink Poodle cocktail lounge—extraordinary for its entertainment line-up and even more so for its unlikely, probably unwitting but significant role in the advancement of Indianapolis's race relations—was razed and forgotten years ago.

———————

That is the way things go in this pleasant Midwestern city where, when it comes to the public narrative, dull wholesomeness smothers strangeness. Here roguishness begins and ends with John Dillinger, who cut such a wide swath (Johnny Depp has played Dillinger in a major motion picture, as has Martin Sheen) there is no suppressing his legacy.

But there are no movies about Tuffy Mitchell (Danny DeVito would have been perfect!). His amazing life—his gambling empire, his bribing of police (successful, until it wasn't), his Pink Poodle, his downfall: it's as if none of it ever happened.

Charles Manson has been similarly erased from Indianapolis history even though he spent some key childhood years here, and the Rev. Jim Jones has been nearly erased even though Jones was a factor in the city for a decade.

And as for the monkeys Jones sold door to door as pets, you wouldn't even know they existed. Jones had his first church here, at 3230 S. Keystone Ave. It was in the early 1950s. Jones was in his early twenties. He imported the monkeys from India and sold them for $29 each. In April 1954, a shipment of seven arrived from Calcutta at the Customs Warehouse in Indianapolis. Four were dead on arrival and the other three nearly dead. Jones balked at the $89 air-freight bill and coldly walked away.

Assistant Customs Collector Eugene J. Okon sent an underling to buy bananas. He mashed up the bananas and mixed in some French brandy he'd confiscated earlier. He fed the goop to the monkeys.

"An hour later," according to the *Indianapolis Star*, "the three animals were able to sit up and chatter softly among themselves."

A government worker going the extra mile. Manson's childhood. A 20-piece dinnerware set in a dead man's Buick. It sounds made-up. But it happened, you can look it up. It's microhistory, small history. It's freaky, obscure bits of information that's easily disregarded. It's not important in that it does not explain, say, the causes of World War I, or who really shot JFK.

Plus, it's gross (dead monkeys?), or at least it lacks dignity (tipsy monkeys?).

Stories like this—bizarre, easily comprehended—could go a long way toward fostering a sense of a collective past. They are the kind of tales that, if anyone knew them, might nurture what is sometimes called "Sense of Place," which is more than simple nostalgia, more than a salve for oldsters. Sense of Place builds civic identity, civic awareness. It builds community. People who know their environs feel more connected, more involved, more like insiders, more like...citizens.

And face it: freaky bits are easier to remember; they are more entertaining.

But Indianapolis, hell-bent to be normal, buries its freaky bits. And so, Sense of Place is in short supply here.

Why does Indianapolis do this? Why does it strive for normalcy? My wife, who lives in Indianapolis but was born and raised in Louisville (where there's a statue of a giant naked dude, a 40-foot reproduction of Michelangelo's *David*, painted gold, on Main Street; and where the slogan of the Louisville Independent Business Alliance is: "Keep Louisville Weird"), has a theory: Louisville's first family, its most influential philanthropists, were and are the worldly, eccentric Browns, who hit the jackpot with Jack Daniels and Early Times. Indianapolis's top burghers, the Lillys, were sober Episcopalians whose big score was insulin.

That's a good theory, but who really knows what the deal is?

———

Everyone knew what the deal was with Tuffy Mitchell, including of course the Indianapolis police, who between 1941 and 1966 arrested Mitchell 40 times. His last legal go-round was in 1964 when prosecutors alleged he was netting $500,000 a year from his numbers racket. The "numbers," a common gambling scheme in the days before gambling was legalized, was in effect a privately-run lottery. People bought tickets from Mitchell's "writers" the way they buy them from convenience store cashiers today.

Mitchell denied the prosecutor's claim he was clearing $500,000 a year. "It's impossible," he said. "I can't count to half a million, let alone make that much money."

But it was obvious he was doing quite well. He and his wife and children lived in a sprawling ranch house on tony North Meridian Street. The house is still standing, but Mitchell's Pink Poodle Lounge, his greatest contribution, was torn down years ago to make room for... a parking lot. No one minded or even noticed.

———

So much of Indianapolis has been torn down, improved. The city is home to one of the largest and best-funded historic preservationist groups in the country. But historic preservationists tend to save serious history like fancy mansions of solid citizens long dead, marvelous old movie theaters, and grand churches, not places with stories so oddball nobody alive ever heard of them or even would believe them.

———

Gone is 208 N. Meridian St., where in 1953 a woman of Irish descent born into poverty and with little formal education, Mary McRee Warble, proprietor of the down-scale Mail Pouch bar, began making and selling doughy, hand-held things called pizzas. She'd got the recipe off a Mail Pouch regular, a hard-drinking old German. The recipe called for lots of Muenster. Mail Pouch patrons had not seen pizza before, and they went crazy for it. Mary McRee Warble's may have been Indianapolis's very first pizza, and Warble was definitely the first person in these parts to start a chain of pizza restaurants. Italianizing her name, Mary called her stores Maria's Pizza, and by 1959 she owned seven of them.

Gone is 14 W. Ohio St., home of Hofmeister's Studio of Physical Culture, Indianapolis's first weight-training facility, and one of the nation's first. It opened in 1936, and in 1951 in walked Hungarian-born Mickey Hargitay. Right off the bat Hargitay, with no previous bodybuilding experience, lifted 215 pounds.

Proprietor Fred Hofmeister, impressed, began working with Hargitay, and by 1955 Hargitay won the "Mr. Universe" contest and soon after that married the movie star Jayne Mansfield and soon after that starred in several not-great movies.

Twenty-five years later young, Austrian-born Arnold Alois Schwarzenegger came to the U.S. with the hope of parlaying his powerful body into something more, as Hargitay had done. "Mickey Hargitay gave hope for someone like myself," Schwarzenegger said upon the former's death in 2006. "When I came to this country in 1968, he was one of the first people I wanted to meet." In the end, Arnold Schwarzenegger topped even Mickey Hargitay: He married well, he made not-great movies, *and* was elected governor of California.

You can live your life without ever knowing what Fred Hofmeister did for Mickey Hargitay and what Hargitay did for both Jayne Mansfield and Arnold Schwarzenegger. You don't need to know the effect on Indianapolis's dining scene of an Irish woman's Eisenhower-era joint venture with a German barfly. Yet now that you do know these things, aren't you glad?

Tuffy Mitchell, the size of an average sixth grader, got the nickname "Tuffy" from his days as an amateur boxer, obviously a bantamweight. He was born in Russia in 1914, a few years before the revolution there. He emigrated to the U.S. and lived most of his adult life in Indianapolis, where he began organizing illegal gambling operations in the 1930s. He was in his twenties.

By the early 1960s, Mitchell's was a huge operation with hundreds of freelance employees selling "numbers" to thousands of optimists, mostly small-timers who rarely put down more than a dollar and sometimes risked as little as a single penny. Most of his customers were African American, and

Mitchell was a common site along Indiana Avenue, the Black commercial district just west of the downtown business district.

In the early 1960s, Indianapolis was Selma-like, its neighborhoods and schools fully segregated. There was a public, city-owned swimming pool, in Douglass Park, reserved just for Blacks (all the others were for whites). Country clubs were off-limits to Blacks.

The downtown business and shopping district may not have been strictly off-limits to Blacks, but Blacks certainly felt unwelcome there. In November 1961 three Black men were refused service at the Hook Drug store at the corner of Meridian and Washington streets. Indianapolis-based Hook was no fringe outlier either but rather the city's dominant drugstore chain, owned and managed by leading locals, chief among them Indianapolis's 1963 "Distinguished Citizen of the Year" August "Bud" Hook.

Also, in 1961, Tuffy Mitchell opened the Pink Poodle at 252 N. Capitol Ave. The building was low, blockish, nondescript, but the address was fascinating. It was in a sort of demilitarized zone; it straddled the border between white Indianapolis and Black Indianapolis. Indiana Avenue was a stone's throw to the west, the heart of downtown was a stone's throw to the east.

As Hook was refusing to serve the three African Americans, Tuffy Mitchell's Pink Poodle Lounge was going the other way. The Poodle hired Black performers, big name entertainers like John Coltrane, Redd Foxx, and Moms Mabley. These were crossover stars who appealed to whites as well as Blacks, and Poodle personnel welcomed customers of both races.

And both races did come, in equal numbers, spared the discomfort of navigating the other's turf by the Poodle's strategic, middle-ground location.

So unusual was such race-mixing that it was considered news. Through the week the Poodle's clientele was "70 percent white, 30 percent Negro," the *Indianapolis News* reported. "On Fridays, it's 70 percent Negro, 30 percent white. And on Saturday, from the matinees through to the wee hours, it's 50-50."

Cocktail lounges don't typically figure into narratives about Civil Rights-era integration, and the Pink Poodle has never before gotten any credit for anything noble, nor has Tuffy Mitchell.

But in all likelihood, this much is true: The Pink Poodle was the first place in Indianapolis where Blacks and whites laughed at the same jokes, tapped their feet to the same rhythms, *partied* together.

You did not *need* to know that.

BIRDS OF PREY

SUSAN NEVILLE

Our house sits on a cul-de-sac in an old ring suburb of Indianapolis. The house is a cape, deceptively small and unadorned. The neighborhood was laid out in the 1970s on what was then a horse farm, and there are still horses grazing, ghostlike, at the end of one of the cul-de-sacs. There are five cul-de-sacs, and no easy way to walk from one to the other. Each of the five noose-shaped streets empties onto what was once a country road and is now the busy road that hems us in. *Dead End* the sign says when you enter our cul-de-sac. *No Outlet* it says on the others.

This area of the city was developed helter-skelter. The people who built these houses had no idea that in a few decades the city's largest malls would be built just a few blocks north and that the city would grow until this neighborhood would be closer to downtown than to the outer edges of the suburbs. When we bought the house, my husband had hoped to plant a large vegetable garden like ones from his childhood, but when there's a hard rain, the back yard becomes a lake of such size and force that there are waves. His garden never stood a chance. During storms, a creek that shows up on city maps as a 'ditch' ends in a kind of raging delta in our yard. Ducks see their reflection beneath them and fly down to what will be a temporary home. The developers also had no idea they had to figure in runoff from the concrete parking lots and roads that now surround us and overwhelm the city's drainage system. The last time it rained, there were two uprooted tree stumps and a swing set along our fence line.

If you leave our cul-de-sac and turn left, you're five minutes away from a mall where there's a Pottery Barn and a West Elm and a Saks Fifth Avenue and a Nordstrom. Turn right and you're at a Home Goods and TJ Maxx. I'm surrounded by so much to crave, to pluck from its corporate stem.

I'm old enough and have lived in the city long enough to remember when there were centuries-old beech trees where the malls are now. I remember the trees being felled and years passing as the ground was broken by bulldozers, backhoes, and graders. I don't know where they came from, really, or who ultimately owns the stores. They just descended and held this part of the city by the throat.

Behind all these stores there's a beautiful stretch of the White River, though the stores and restaurants have their backs turned to it and you have to park in front of the stores and walk past loading docks and dumpsters to get a glimpse of water. It's one of the first places people look when some-one's gone missing. This is where the birds of prey now build their nests.

My husband, a farmer in his heart, keeps our birdfeeders filled all winter. The first thing he does when he gets home from work, before coming inside, is to take cups of sunflower seed and thistle to the feeders. In the winter, he replenishes the suet. In the summer, he keeps three hummingbird feeders filled with simple syrup. We've watched blue robin's eggs hatch in the dogwood tree outside our dining room window, and sometimes the yellow finches swarm from tree to flower to feeder like butterflies.

My husband also keeps a stack of rocks to throw at the hawks when they hover. He was a pitcher for his high school baseball team and has a good arm. He can get just close enough to scare them off but not to hurt them. Of course, I tell him, if he didn't feed the smaller birds, the larger ones would stay away. There's the irony, he says.

One day a Cooper's Hawk the size of a small eagle tried to get into our living room through the screen window, and after that, the hawk took to sitting on the deck rails or the mailbox early evening. When the hawk was around, the entire neighborhood went quiet. First, the small birds would sound a warning and then go quiet and then the cicadas and then all the people and the dogs, reacting to the silence, would go quiet as well. It was like the moment in a theatre right after the previews end and before the movie begins when the hands in all the popcorn bags and the sound of munching, even your own breathing, seem so loud that hands and mouths are held in position until the fresh blast of color and sound from the screen allows the eating and breathing to begin again.

That hawk is some hawk's child, I told my husband when he threw rocks at it, and of course, he agreed. That it needed nourishment was irrefutable. But not *his* birds, my husband said, not while he was watching. The poor chickadees, he said. The cardinals. The nuthatch. And the babies. Why do the hawks hover during nesting season, when it's not even sporting?

Ah, and there's the question.

Now and then I'll have a moment when the sacrificial nature of reality—of predator and prey, matter and antimatter, energy being transformed

THE INDIANAPOLIS ANTHOLOGY

in the process of eating, all of it violent—will strike me as a kind of grace. Something in me will see the hawk with the finch and imagine it multiplied by trillions upon trillions of daily sacraments as though there is nothing else but this, and I will say yes, this is right, this is beautiful. But then I'll hear the scream of the finch in the kite's mouth or I'll step on a shard of glass and feel the pain, the vision's gone, and all of it is horrible again, the universe nothing but one vicious hungry mouth pitted against the will for survival. And so I cheer the suicidally courageous robin swooping at the hawk, getting him away from her nest, watching the hawk glide off through the jeweled sky, over the back yards, like a stealth bomber. He will return, we know. Oh yes, he will return.

———————

My husband and I met when we were eighteen years old, college freshmen. We were computer dates for the freshman mixer. We both loved the Temptations, and we think that's why the computer fixed us up. That, and our height. Computers couldn't handle too much subtlety then; they spit out data punch cards like vending machine candy.

He had received a scholarship for first-generation college students. It paid for his tuition and room and board, and he worked pulling weeds for a landscaper in the summer. When he came to my dorm, I hid behind a potted plant until I saw the young man I'd been matched with. He was frighteningly handsome and, as it turned out, would be one of the smartest people I would ever know. And kind. Luckily for me, he didn't know any of that. We were both shy. We both had parents who were disabled. We thought that's why the universe put us together. His mother wept when they dropped him off at school and she wept when he told her, four years later, that we were getting married. That's it for me, she thought. He's got him a wife. I had swooped him up and away from her. I had wept the first month of school, homesick, until I met her son. It seems we traded tears.

———————

My husband comes from generations of southern Indiana farmers.

It's important that when I say farm, you don't imagine vast fields of one crop. Those are industrial farms. When I say farm, I mean you grow what you and your family need to live and perhaps a bit more to sell. And while everything is a choice, this was not a choice among many but one born of poverty and tradition.

When I first met my husband, he lived in a rural area outside of Columbus, Indiana. This was not the farm his family had lived on for all those generations. I would only hear stories of the family farm but would never get to see it directly because, by the time my husband was born, it no longer existed. Still, I got to know the names of the horses and neighbors, heard the stories of the shack in the woods where the young men went to drink and play cards. And I heard stories of the town called Kansas.

A month after the attack on Pearl Harbor, the United States government requisitioned more than 40,000 acres of land in southern Indiana to build the Army base known as Camp Atterbury. My husband's family homestead was among those acres.

In addition to family homes, included in the requisitioned land were fifteen cemeteries, five schools, numerous churches, and the entire town of Kansas, all of which were obliterated. My husband's father's post office address was Kansas. His father and uncles and aunts and grandparents' addresses were as well. The entire family, and all the others located within those 40,000 acres, had ten days to move out.

When the civilians were gone, the Army burned the houses and stacks of cherry wood ready for market, burnt the crops, moved four of the five cemeteries, bulldozed the five schools and all of the churches to build barracks and training fields. The camp served as a staging area, and for a while, it housed over 10,000 German and Italian prisoners of war. The prisoners of war built a chapel on the base. The Italians used berries and their own blood to tint the frescoes.

An Indiana history site says the Army *bought* the land from the farmers, but no one was *paid* in this purchase, at least not the families. There's no anger about this that I could ever tell, just sadness. There were far worse uprootings in Europe at the time and the young men were all about to be uprooted nonetheless: drafted or sent to work in the factories.

Once a year, on Memorial Day weekend, descendants of the families get a bus tour through the still-working Army camp. It's the only time the off-limits parts of the base are open to civilians. We usually go. Much of the land is now uninhabitable, filled with unexploded ordnance; those acres are used for target practice. There are practice sniper towers and fake Middle Eastern villages with roofless homes for the soldiers to practice capturing, and there are tank tracks in the dusty roads. Along the roads, there are pop-up enemy soldiers like the ducks at State Fair shooting galleries. The enemy soldiers are dressed in headscarves and robes. You shoot them and they pop back up so you can practice shooting them again.

When the former landowners' bus drives through, all the shooting stops for those few hours so we can visit the remaining cemeteries. But during the week, you can hear the bombs going off in Camp Atterbury in towns miles away. Sometimes the vibrations are so bad that knick-knacks fall off of end tables.

The place itself is beautiful, rolling land, difficult to farm, but most of the families who lived there had their roots, in the wayback, in Scotland and Ireland and in the nearer wayback in North Carolina high country, so the hills had seemed relatively familiar and easy and there were enough flat acres for small farms. It's easy to see why the government chose this place. Aside from its location in the center of the country, with this land, you could practice bombing both hilly terrain and flatland. You could rise up from the hills in helicopters and there was still enough space to build landing fields for fixed-wing planes. The last time we took our tour through the camp and all the guns were silenced, there were drones, quiet and eerie, flying overhead like raptors.

My husband's father, his home now gone, was disabled early in the war. He contracted tuberculosis while building fence in Hawaii and was shipped back to the states where he had to lie in hospital for seven years. Some of those years were in a hospital in what is now The Presidio in San Francisco and some of them in Texas and some in a sanitarium in Kentucky. He lost one lung and several ribs, and his chest was caved in where the lung had been. As long as he lived, he was short of breath. If not for the tuberculosis, my husband points out, he would have gone with his unit to the Philippines where, if he'd lived, he likely would have been in the death march to Bataan.

During the war, my husband's mother volunteered at the sanitarium which was near her farm in Science Hill, Kentucky, bringing ripe tomatoes and blackberries to the soldiers and sitting by their bedsides. That's where she met my husband's father, the man without a lung. As it turned out, his name was Kenneth like a beloved brother who'd died in childhood. This Kenneth was also fragile, pale, and handsome as a film star. This Kenneth she could save. Of course, she married him. Together they had one child, a son, and they named him Kenneth as well. That third Kenneth is my husband.

After their marriage, my mother-in-law spent her days lifting heavy sacks of corn and feed in a small grocery. Most of the customers were the rural poor and the migrant workers who came through during harvests. My mother-in-law grew to know the migrants, to watch their children grow as they came through year after year, first with their parents and then by themselves. She knew their family names and what happened to them.

The migrant workers lived in old trailers with no running water. There was one outside pump for a group of families. They picked worms off the tobacco as she had when she was young. They picked the strawberries and detasseled the corn. Except for the moving around, she knew that life. After work, my mother-in-law walked home and cooked and gardened alongside her husband. One of the migrant children who came through her store is now an Indianapolis poet, a friend of mine.

One reason we live in this particular house is because the yard brings back memories for my husband. When I see him get on the riding mower and mow the grass, I know he feels his father's old tractor beneath him and sees his father digging up potatoes with a fork and he remembers what it felt like to ride a pony through the woods and to take a shower in a washhouse and the scent of the warm kitchen when his mother canned beans and, sweet Jesus, fresh peaches and grape and strawberry jam.

When he rototills a patch to make a garden, he remembers the rototiller his father and his uncles shared. He would have liked, if he had his druthers, to live out in the country again.

Last night I asked my husband, after having known him for almost fifty years, what it is he used to know how to do that he doesn't know now. I thought it would have been farming or fishing or canning, but the things he knew then he still knows, he said. He just doesn't do them. He doesn't romanticize the way he grew up. By the time he was in high school, he was embarrassed by his poverty. When someone gave him a ride home, he'd have them drop him off at the bottom of the hill. This is not to say that he was embarrassed by his parents. He loved and respected them.

The things he never learned at all are the things that haunt him.

His father could fix a tractor with baling wire and twine. He was good with engines, was what they called a "shade tree mechanic." My husband never learned any of this. He never paid attention, he said, because those were different times and his family made it clear he was made for different things.

His father butchered hogs. In the fall he'd string a hog up to a tree and gut it. The hog bled out. There were other steps, but he never learned them. You don't get attached to hogs, my husband explains to me. Believe me, he said. There was always an uncle or great uncle to help with the butchering. Basil or Bryce, he says, those people who didn't have jobs.

I don't remember Basil and Bryce, I say to him, though I remember their names and I don't know anything about people who never have jobs by choice. His grandmother had a string of brothers and sisters, most of whom were named after herbs or gemstones (Ruby and Pearl and Beryl and Anise) and several of whom hadn't worked at paying jobs since they were kicked off the army base. No one seemed to think this was odd. They were doing something and they were told by the federal government they couldn't do it, so they didn't. So perhaps it wasn't by choice.

Sometimes they would take the ponies over to Bryce's to graze, my husband says, and his dad and Bryce would talk about nothing for a while. Bryce still lived in a shack without running water. They'd pump water from the well and take it out to the ponies in buckets. If you went on down that road, my husband says, my Grandpa and Grandma King had a small farm and on Sunday mornings we would go down there and fish and eat bologna sandwiches and it was the happiest time in my life. I was three or four, he said. They had given the land to Bryce and Basil. Neither Bryce nor Basil nor his other grandfather, Grandpa Long, had a job, but it never occurred to him that they should have. Not at the time. Grandma Long had a stereopticon! While Grandpa Long was a mean son of a bitch, my husband said, it didn't matter. They'd all go out and gather hickory nuts. There were a lot of sunfish in the pond, and they'd fish. They'd listen to Hank Williams and my husband's father would smoke cigars. Sometimes, before his mother joined a church, they would drink beer and whiskey. When my husband's mother joined a church, their Sundays changed forever, and my husband never quite forgave her for that.

The church people came out into the country and converted her, snatched her up, so the whole family had to go and be told, every Sunday, that hell was a real place they were going to unless they came to the front of the church and were dunked in the baptismal pool. My husband did this at thirteen, even though he didn't really believe any of it. After that, my husband's father couldn't have a beer with his brothers, or play cards with them, or take his son fishing on Sunday morning or on a visit to the farm to view the stereopticon.

I've thought a lot, over the years, about Camp Atterbury and don't think I've ever fully understood the cost to the families who were displaced, which means I know nothing about much of human history, which is the story of forced migrations.

Everyone knew everyone in Kansas, though when I think about it now the everyone they knew became clearly demarcated by the artificial boundaries of what would become the army camp that displaced them. Inside the lines was one country, outside the lines another. Outside those lines was a strange country.

It's easy to romanticize the life inside those lines, to divide the world into before and after the Fall. But as my husband pointed out to me, it was such an isolated area before the war: cousins marrying distant cousins, everyone a Neville or a Coe or a Long or a Miller. No one left. Few finished high school. They were intelligent, lively, people and it was the only world they knew. They might still be there if not for the uprooting.

After the war, they scattered. And by the time the next generation came along some of their children founded banks and engine companies and doughnut factories; some became doctors and politicians and Silicon Valley entrepreneurs. There were both losses and gains, but their DNA sweetened with other DNA, they made their way into the world. This happens after wars, this migration and this mixing. It's just a thing that happens. The genetic pool swirls and some strands are reinforced and some win out over others.

When historical trauma affects your family personally it takes two to three generations to forget, though the attempts at forgetting begin right away. As long as someone is alive to tell the story firsthand, the story is alive: colored by stages of anger, grief, and wonder; undergoing subtle changes as the effects are suffered, understood, integrated, registered, passed on. It's possible that the trauma never really goes away, that only the origins are forgotten.

During the first world war, my husband's great-grandfather lost a daughter to the Spanish Flu, sons to the fighting. Historical trauma intruded into the life he'd made there in Kansas. One day he went out to the barn and tied one end of a rope to a rafter and one to his neck. He stood on a baby carriage and jumped off, "flying into eternity," the newspapers said.

Sometimes when we go back through the camp on Memorial Day an old man will see something, a favorite oak tree, say, now riddled with bullet holes, and you can see the enduring sadness at the loss of all the things, both natural and human-made, that make a home.

In the days after he was kicked off his farm, my husband's grandfather, son of a suicide, found work on the farm of a wealthy man named Harry Hill. What was left of the family moved into a house on the back of Hill's property. Right after the move, they got the news about Kenneth's tuberculosis. So, in one year they lost a farm, a way of life, and now had a son near death. They would soon lose one daughter to marriage and two more sons, as they were drafted immediately after their graduation from high school.

And all the time, they worried about the fate of their oldest son, Kenneth, the son with tuberculosis. News of his health was sporadic, not reliable. They were told repeatedly that he was near death, and one day the family received a telegram from the Army saying that Kenneth had died and asking what they wanted done with the body. They lived with the knowledge of his death for over a week before discovering the telegram had been sent to them in error.

Within a few months, Hill sold the farm, leaving the grandfather without work again or a place to live. Hill offered him a job in a veneer mill he owned. My husband's grandfather had no other choice. He took the job in the mill, but they had to move again to a house outside Edinburgh, Indiana.

For a man used to farming, millwork was hot and repetitious, claustrophobic and dark, the factory filled with the whining of saws and the smell of vats of vinegar used to soften wood. He started developing headaches.

As my husband's aunt, the youngest child and the only one left at home during that time, tells the story, on a hot August evening her father came home with a pint of ice cream to share with her. After that, he went inside but she vividly remembers him leaving the house again. Her mother was pumping water at the well on the west side of the house, and she saw her father exit from the east, dressed in his overalls and cap and carrying a rifle.

"He edged around the east side of the house, making certain to stay out of Mom's sight," Aunt Shirley said. She assumed he was sneaking off to go hunting. At that point in her parents' lives, they weren't talking to one another, the marriage itself a victim of the forced evacuation, so Shirley wasn't surprised by the sneaking off.

At dusk, Shirley went with her mother to close the barn door. While they didn't farm, they still kept cows, and earlier that evening the cows had been put up for the night but somehow the door had come partially open. The cows were crowding against it now, trying to escape. Shirley and her mother struggled to push the cows back inside and bolt the door.

It turned dark. The father had left with a gun. He hadn't returned.

My mother began to grow agitated, Shirley remembers, and she called relatives in Columbus. After securing their promise to come to their house, she accidentally left the handset off the hook. The two of them went upstairs and sat on the bed in the dark of the upstairs bedroom. Shirley heard voices downstairs, unreal and disembodied, voices of people on the party line.

They waited in the dark. When relatives arrived from town, they searched and eventually discovered the body in the barn, lying inside the door. My husband's grandfather had shot himself with the .22 caliber rifle. It was his body that had made the door so hard to close. The notice in the paper was eerily similar to the notice of his own father's death in a barn, two decades before.

The next day, the casket was brought into the house and placed in the living room. Because of the war, the children were scattered and some, including my husband's father, were not able to attend the funeral.

I don't understand why we love and have to die, or even why the universe requires our suffering, but I've lost both my parents and several aunts and uncles and all of my grandparents and I think I know what mourning is. But on one day to have the long conversation of marriage end, to see the one you've lived your adult life with die. That, for some reason, I can't, don't want to, imagine.

One day fifteen years ago my husband's parents were sitting side by side on the front porch and the next day my husband's father collapsed and my husband's mother ran into the house to call 911 then went back outside and tried to rouse him.

The tart cherry trees were loaded with ripe red cherries they had intended to pick. The jam jars were washed and waiting on the kitchen table. When the ambulance arrived, the EMT picked her husband up and slammed him down on the wooden deck, trying to get his heart to beat again. They did it more than once, slamming his dead body on the deck, in front of the pink impatiens. That night we all drove down from Indianapolis and put the jam jars in the basement.

Three years later my mother-in-law would die as well, in the hospital, of pneumonia. And that was the end of that story.

And here's my story:

My senior year in college I fell into a depression so deep and so new to me I thought I'd rather die than live if adult life would feel like this. Because my husband was a psych major, and he continued to love me through this time, I offered myself up for studies that year. An almost psychotically depressed person, I was. Real and in the flesh. Unmedicated. Ripe for study. As part of the study, I was hooked up to biofeedback machines that traced my brain waves and promised to teach me how to create the calming ones. Your brain waves, the psychologist told me, are odd. I looked at the print-out. There were the jittery nervous waves that hugged the bottom of the chart but easily interspersed were the tallest of the looping ones, the ones hard to create outside of sleep, floating along above them, and I said that's about right. That's how my brain feels to me.

When I write now, I feel those waves. I feel as though my brain is operating at two different heights or frequencies simultaneously. One part is running along the ground, quivering, rodent-like, part of the grass, the stones, the dirt, the worms where they're working, the insects, the fungus that's lacing the fallen leaves of the dogwood tree: everything close up, magnified, quick. The other part of my brain is flying above, effortless and quiet, rapturous, watching where the rodent goes, waiting to strike whatever it finds, or the rodent itself, one thing feeding on the other. It's hard to explain what I mean, but the rapture and the skittishness exist at once, make the same moves, always connected to one another, one the senses and one the mind.

Somehow I broke through the terrifying twilight of that time and have learned to live in the world with all its light and shadows. My husband and I live together in this house and we love each other and our children deeply. At some point, too, I gave myself to writing and it feeds me. Ultimately, that's my only story, but there are costs. Because I want to say that I know, I deeply know, my husband's family story isn't mine to tell and I know, I deeply know, how much I owe that family and how telling that story that is not mine to tell might hurt them in ways I'm not even aware of. Not future generations but the ones who are still alive, the ones who experienced it. It is their story still. But I am what I was born to be. And so, here I am at my desk. Talons sharp. Telling it.

PUPPIES 4 SALE

JIM POWELL

No takers since the mid-afternoon drunk who'd crunched the curb when he pulled over. The little dogs had moaned and scratched the travel crate in fear. Monte first refused to sell to him, then figured business was business. "Puppies 4 Sale" his sign offered. Total for two days—five dogs sold, three to go. Monte sat on the concrete steps, one arm rested on the metal mesh while the other waved a cigarette in the air whenever a car slowed. Traffic was thin on State Street today, his last with this litter. Food cost him the humiliation of scavenging scraps at Kate's Café or behind the Village Pantry east on Prospect. If they didn't sell, after dark he'd drown the dogs—he refused to call them puppies except with clients.

Few of those nearby though the neighborhood stayed busy, rehabs and new restaurants a few blocks over near Fountain Square, and especially down at the corner where the latest renovation picked up speed. Monte saw the money guy who'd bought three of the four corners—the brick buildings—surveying the exterior handiwork on the one that neared completion. The next block north he watched his once friend Sandi, now a red-haired meth whore in ripped jeans, wiggling her scrawny hips beside a bus stop as if some stranger might descend and buy. But her skanky tit-tats and wobbly platforms were no more enticing than her bad teeth. Monte wondered how a man could allow his dick to enter such decay. He'd told her "no" several times since he'd gotten off the meth himself after two despairing weeks dabbling with it. While he couldn't say he felt in all ways cured yet, at least he could enjoy the sunshine on his bare arms without scratching or squinting to avoid seeing the world around him for what it was. Eyes open it was pretty damned crappy, but the neighborhood was his reality, his life.

The dogs whimpered and he almost broke down to scratch one little nose pushed through the wire. The renovator man paced toward him as if measuring the empty lot between his building and Monte's house. "Shush up," Monte told the dogs. "You'd eat good with this guy, believe me." He gentled the carrier like a cradle then stood.

He couldn't remember the money man's name but tried to smile. About thirty like Monte, he'd power-washed the ancient two-story so the brick came clean and sharp-edged. He'd put in new doors—at the back wooden ones with mosaic patterns and, on the front, silvery scroll work and hinges shaped like Arabian swords. Above that door he'd placed a limestone wolf's head. The bastioned battlement around the roof's edge made the place look like a fortress.

Mr. Money hollered, "Hey, brother," giving a two-fingered salute. His step quickened and Monte remembered the name—Travis, like a traveling salesman. His work clothes, cowhide carpenter pants and suspenders over a flannel shirt, remained unstained even in the heat. But at least he was doing a lot of the building work himself, so they had something in common. Last year, when Monte lost the go-pher job at the woodworking plant he'd hoped would lead to an apprenticeship, he got right back to work building the "kennel" behind the house he'd inherited from his mother, his single legacy. Only his ex-girlfriend Vicky "helped." They even made a stab at putting up a high wood fence until he realized that if the posts weren't cemented the whole thing would fall. He realized that, of course, only when it happened.

Travis put out his hand and Monte took it tentatively. "I got some cute puppies here, mister... Travis," he stammered, embarrassed at the guy's quick shake and dismissal.

Travis peered into the cage, hopefully attracted by their unusual features. The dogs yelped in relief from their boredom. Monte hoped they sounded like good property guardians.

Monte had no idea what work was still going on inside the building but knew that Travis also bought Sammy's Saloon nearby, long closed despite its notoriety as a '20s honky-tonk speakeasy. Signs of the past were easily forgotten in these parts. Kitty-corner from the reno, a carved limestone "F. & A. M." still ID'ed the three-story Masonic lodge that now housed a used clothes store and crappy studio apartments.

One of the tenants there, a puffy woman in a Black Sabbath tee-shirt, neared them pushing a stroller. She said, "Say 'hi' to the neighbors, honey," and both Monte and Travis nodded to the toddler, who sported a mullet. The tyke rode bare-chested and surly looking, concentrating on the Popsicle he grasped like a prize. The dogs quieted and the kid said nothing. The woman shrugged and walked on.

Travis, like Monte, barely contained his laughter. "Man, that's some hairdo on a baby." Travis giggled into his hand. "Our neighbors," he said. "At least until next October."

So, the Masonic building would be emptied and redone, too. Travis had supposedly encouraged the going-out-of-business sale at the Used Tire

Depot that filled the fourth corner. Who knew what so-called progress might develop there if the public housing project under debate for that block fell through? Restaurants he'd never afford or a Starbucks for people with time to waste.

Monte smiled as if the idea of change made him happy and Travis asked him to bring one of the dogs out into the light. Monte fiddled with the lock and their tongues gooed-up his knuckles. His skin was still touchy after four weeks clean. Thank God he'd wised up before he ended like Sandi. He grabbed one of the dogs by its scruff and closed the door on the other two. "This one's got the spirit."

Travis petted between the dog's big ears. Monte figured he might not want as much fight in his dogs as most people in the neighborhood. "But the patience of an angel, too," quoting something his mom once said about him.

Monte held the little dog so its legs kicked. Its coat shone in the sunshine, short yellow-brown fur. Wind up around forty-fifty pounds, but tough with shepherd and terrier in the mix. "Here, you hold him. Cute guy's not a biter."

Travis took a step back and eyed the dog all around as if examining a statue. "I need a watchdog for the building while we finish the upstairs' lofts." He waved his hand back and forth in the dog's face. To see how the eyes tracked, Monte guessed.

He bounced the dog a little, to shake out more reaction, but it cooed and drooled, not a single yip or nip. "Oh, he's gotta lot of life, mister. Just woke up from a nap. "Full shepherd."

Travis tightened his mouth. "Part maybe." He petted the dog's rump, then pulled his hand away and wiped it on his thigh.

"Or I've got another bitch ready to drop that's part pit bull." Another month before he could sell any of those potential killers. He'd regretted borrowing the ill-tempered stud when he witnessed its aggressive mating.

Travis chuckled. "I don't think so, bud." He scanned down State in Sandi's direction as if the next block might make good property for him. He grimaced when he caught sight of the girl, who gave a come-hither wave and bent over a bit so her tits showed white amidst the ink. "Christ," he muttered. "Maybe I should hire *her*. No one would dare break in on that."

Sandi took the attention as an invitation and staggered toward them, scratching her arm. Monte tensed. She wasn't a bad person, he reminded himself, or once hadn't been. Christ, they'd been kids together at McKinley Elementary when the new building opened. In fourth grade, she'd kissed him by the swing set before she moved on to more experienced boys and other cities. Been a hairdresser or something. She'd come back home only to be kicked out by her parents. He wished he didn't know where she lived.

"Hey, Monte," she crooned. "Cute little puppies, huh, mister." Her words tripped out over ragged teeth. Red scabs dotted her cheeks and neck like measles. "Buy me a puppy, mister, and we'll be your friends for life." Even her girlish giggle mocked the real thing.

She reached toward Travis' arm, but he pulled back. "Sorry, sister, nothing for you." He drew himself up. "Except some advice."

Sandi raised her eyebrows and chuckled and Monte worried Travis might slap her. He stood in case he needed to step between them.

"You can get help at the Center," Travis said, referring to the new community center a few blocks north across Washington Street where renovation work continued—of people as well as buildings—making that neighborhood feel better, at least for the moment. "All you have to do is walk in the door and ask."

Sandi snorted and glared, but at Monte, not Travis who turned his back on her. She pushed her lips together in a fake kiss. "You assholes have a nice day, you hear." She spat on the ground toward Monte. "You got cute puppies, Monte. Glad you made some friends." She scowled then stalked away.

Travis stretched his shoulders. "Don't think I'll be hiring *that* for anything." He again scanned the dog. "And I can't use your dog, either. Sorry, buddy."

Monte sat down and brought the dog into his lap. "But maybe you could hire me." He straightened. "I'm tougher than I look." He scratched behind the dog's ears. "I'm about done with this puppy business." It was true. He was making bread money, not mortgage. He didn't want to go back to working the pick-up crews with men in worse shape than him or selling dope. Working for this asshole would be a new start. He restrained the wriggling dog easily, his muscle tone rebuilding, more beefed up considering his distance from poor Sandi's fall.

Travis towered over him, scanning Monte like he had the dog. "Dude, you are skin and bones." He scanned Monte's house as well. "But maybe you could sell this place to me. Must be a lot for you to take care of."

Monte thought his house not so bad, paint chipped and shingles faded but gutters unbent. Plenty around here had weathered worse. His mother had put pride into it, and their neighborhood where people looked out for one another. Now, most of her generation were dead or moved. It didn't matter. He had no place else to go and the mortgage crisis made his lender forgiving, seemingly unaware that investors like Travis might take interest in the decay.

"Nah, I been in here three years since my Mom died. And this is my neighborhood since I was a kid." Travis wasn't giving, so he might as well push back. "Besides, you Fountain Square big shots think you're improving the neighborhood so much, my house might really be worth a few bucks to you before long."

Travis snickered. "Oh, so happy to give you folks some hope." He reached out—Monte feared to punish his insolence—but only tapped the dog's head and turned away.

Good riddance, Monte thought. Whose renewal was this urban renewal stuff anyway? The guy hadn't dealt with despair one second of his life. Monte opened the crate and scooted the dog back inside. He wondered how soon the whole corner would advertise "lofts" or "flats." The business renovations seemed never to end, and the little houses built on half-lots in the early 1900s were thinned out by foreclosure and demolition all the way over to Fountain Square.

The dogs shuffled around on their over-sized paws. Monte rocked the cage and squinted after Travis who stood in the weedy lot reading a newly planted plastic sign titled "New Public Housing—Hearing Sunday." He pulled the invitation from the ground, rolled it into a wand, and used the metal stumps to poke the ground. Then he sniffed the air.

He called back to Monte. "Man, I can smell your dogs from here. You're gonna have to do something about that." Travis gave a thumbs-up and nodded as if he assumed Monte's agreement. He turned on his heels like a soldier, marched to his building, and disappeared inside.

Now that Monte smelled for it, he found plenty of dog in the air—so what? He rattled the crate and the three dogs whimpered at his anger. "Like hell I'll get rid of you," he whispered.

Up the street, Sandi sat against a spindly tree. Weeds nearly covered her body, her once-pretty face showing like a dried flower. Monte squinted. They were all refugees in their own neighborhood. He couldn't offer his spare room, but he'd walk her to the community center. Otherwise, she might disappear into the haze he'd almost entered until the litter's birth returned his sense of responsibility. He'd watched their mother nurse them, her irritation growing until Monte started to wean them. Brushed them. Petted them. Scratched their ears and in the empty lot buried the runt that died.

Monte wiped his eyes, sore and moist. He rocked the carrier and the puppies woofed. He talked back to them, promising that even if he had to move, he'd find each one a good home.

RUTH LILLY'S HOUSE

NORMAN MINNICK

Having just won
the prestigious
Ruth Lilly Prize,
Kay Ryan asked
if I knew where
the celebrated
philanthropist lived.
We drove up
to the estate,
which is known
as Twin Oaks
and is difficult
to see from the road.
The gate was open
so I drove in
and pulled up
to the house
in my Honda Civic
LX with two
missing hubcaps.
"What's the plan
if someone comes
out?" I asked.
"We don't look
intimidating,"
she assured me,
"But to be safe
pretend we are lost."

MOURNING AT THE MLK-RFK MEMORIAL

DAN CARPENTER

(17th and Broadway, Indianapolis, where street crime struck my friends)

Anybody here
sees my old friend Martin
must be looking up
and away
from the life and death
of this broken-promise land
on these nights
when lifelessness flows like water
over the weed stumps and rubble
over martyrs in metal on high
over a marker the artist
forged from melted-down guns
Anybody here on foot
alone and wary or
in a pack prowling
—non-violent in hope
or in the breach—
is on no Selma march
on these nights
in this day of dreamlessness
Martin up there
who got there with Bobby
not down here with you
where the Movement's just history these days Brother
now you keep movin' or you be too

Anybody here
Anybody here my friend
best look around
be gone

2014

THROUGH OUR EYES

TATJANA REBELLE

Indianapolis
From Haughville to Lawrence
Broad Ripple to Clifton
Devington to Mars Hill
Neighborhoods built by residents and renamed by gentrification
Grocery stores turned breweries
Closed schools turned condos
Retails shops with empty windows symbolizing someone's dream unfulfilled
Pothole ridden streets turn daily commutes into obstacle courses
Fear based legislation leaving countless to feel unprotected, hiding their
    identities to blend in despite their own happiness
Displacement is rich in its history
Miami land fertilized by remnants of strange fruit
You can hear the whispers of history and dreams of the future if you close
    your eyes
Listen…
Indianapolis speaks in tongues of languages of distant lands
An abuela singing songs from her childhood creating new memories in her
    new home
French, Swahili, Burmese, Arabic and more, syllables dancing intertwining
    with the wind
African drums pulsating through walls infecting you with the spirit of
    motherlands
Echoes of Indiana Ave resonating from the Box turned Sunday night pulpit,
    to the Coalyard, bending with the whims of the Monon and syncopating
    to marches of the Fort's past.
Witness…
Love resonating from street to street as the rainbow illuminates smiles of
    everyone it waves to
Saturdays where Community Controlled Food Initiatives and farmers
    markets bring fresh food to fill the bellies of all its people, even those too
    many have forgotten about
Rebuilt Ruins absorbing laughter reminding us that the spirit of joy is what
    unites us

Asante's children creating legacy through arts and theater, passing down
   creativity to all those that cross their path
Muslim Youth Collectively uniting to bring change within themselves and
   their community
Watch as a neighborhood GRoEs and connects through each open bite and by
   reclaiming the throne others have tried to remove
Indianapolis
You are so much more than your past
You are full of stories untold
Stories that can meld into your promising future
From the barber shops to the front porches
From the coffeeshops to the dinner tables
But you must listen and witness the greatness that you can be and already are
Indianapolis, you are because we are
We are because you are home

CONTRIBUTORS

Desiree Arce is an Argentinean self-published author. She started writing at the age of seven and won different writing competitions in her home-town. She moved to Indianapolis ten years ago and currently lives with her husband and two boys on the North Side of the city. She published her first book *Los pájaros que cantan* in 2011. Most recently she graduated from Marian University with a Business degree.

Michael Brockley lives in Muncie, Indiana. His poems have appeared in *Tipton Poetry Journal, The Flying Island, Gargoyle,* and *Visiting Bob: Poems Inspired by the Life and Work of Bob Dylan.*

A'Lelia Bundles, who grew up in Indianapolis, is the author of *On Her Own Ground: The Life and Times of Madam C. J. Walker.* Her stories about Walker and other topics also appear on her websites at www.aleliabundles. com and www.madamcjwalker.com.

A poet, fiction writer, blogger and freelance journalist born and residing in Indianapolis, **Dan Carpenter** has published poems and stories in many journals and is the author of four books.

Jared Carter's most recent book of poems, *The Land Itself,* is from Monon-gahela Books in Morgantown, West Virginia. He lives on the Near-Eastside of Indianapolis.

Malachi "A+scribe" Carter is a Far East Side Indy artist. He describes his writing as "those inner-city school field trips to a Broadway musical (before, during, and after)." He probably does too many things as a rapper, poet, podcaster, teacher, youth minister, Masters student and photographer, but he just cannot seem to stick to wearing just one hat; they all are so dope!

Bryan Furuness is the author of a couple of novels, *The Lost Episodes of Revie Bryson* and *Do Not Go On.* His most recent anthology is *An Indiana Christmas.* He lives in Indianapolis, where he teaches at Butler University.

Dan Grossman is a freelance journalist based in Carmel. He is the former arts editor at *NUVO,* and has published frequently in *NUVO,* and a research assistant at the IUPUI Arts and Humanities Institute. He is the author of the novel *Rogue Elephants: A Novel of the Peace Corps,* available on Lulu.com.

Terrance Hayes is the author of *To Float in the Space Between: A Life and Work in Conversation with the Life and Work of Etheridge Knight* (Wave Books, 2018), *American Sonnets for My Past and Future Assassin,* a finalist for the National Book Award for poetry, *How to Be Drawn,* which received a 2016 NAACP Image Award for Poetry, *Lighthead,* which won the 2010 National Book Award for poetry, and three other award-winning poetry collections. His honors include a National Endowment for the Arts Fellowship, a Guggenheim Fellowship, and a 2014 MacArthur Fellowship. He is the poetry editor at the *New York Times Magazine* and also teaches at the University of Pittsburgh.

Angela Herrmann is an Indiana-born writer, photographer, and gardener. She is a silver-level Advanced Master Gardener and has earned certificates in agroecology and permaculture.

Writing for the *Indianapolis Star/USA Today/*Gannett, **Will Higgins** covered, among other things, the war in Iraq, KKK cross burnings, the career of the Midwest's youngest pimp, the life of a two-foot-tall Chinese man who became a small Indiana town's richest citizen and high-level dope dealing by certain 1980s Indy 500 drivers. Higgins unearthed the source of the FBI's dead-serious and years-long investigation into the supposedly dirty lyrics of the 1960s pop song "Louie Louie." He invented the sport of Linear Bocce and serves as commissioner of the American Association of Linear Bocce. He makes the occasional art installation, such as the "American Society of Presidential Urine Collectors," as seen at the Indianapolis Museum of Contemporary Art in 2016. He is a nationally ranked tennis player.

Allyson Horton is the author of *Quick Fire,* her first collection of poetry (Third World Press Foundation). She received her MFA in Creative Writing from Butler University. Her poems have appeared in *It Was Written: Poetry Inspired by Hip Hop, Not Our President, Brilliant Flame!* and *Black Panther: Paradigm Shift or Not?* Her work has most recently been published in *The Indianapolis Review* and literary magazine *African Voices* (NY). Currently, she teaches and resides in her hometown of Indianapolis.

Dr. Terri Jett was born in Oakland and raised in Richmond, California and earned a Ph.D. in Public Policy and Public Administration from Auburn University. She is a Professor of Political Science, an affiliate faculty member of the Gender, Women & Sexuality Studies Program and Special Assistant to the Provost for Diversity and Inclusivity at Butler University. Dr. Jett is President of the Board of the American Civil Liberties Union of Indiana and also serves as a Trustee on the Board of the Indianapolis Public Library and is a member of the Indiana Humanities Board and the Indianapolis Local Public Improvement Bond Bank Board of Directors.

Dr. Darolyn "Lyn" Jones serves as the Education Outreach Director for the Indiana Writers Center overseeing the Building a Youth Public Memoir Program. Lyn is also an assistant teaching professor in the Department of English at Ball State University. Lyn is passionate about literacy, story, and social and educational justice and has committed her thirty years of professional life to those topics. Lyn writes and publishes about community writing engagement in peer-reviewed scholarly journals. She is the educational author of a top-selling series book titled, *Painless Reading Comprehension*, co-author of *Memory Workshop* with Barbara Shoup, the editor for a digital literary magazine, *Rethinking Children's & YA Lit: Read for Change*, the editor for the 409 Press, a creative writing Indie Ball State press, an editor for the children's book series, the *Neon Tiki Tribe*, and one of the editors for the independent press, INwords Publications. Lyn has edited and published five different memoir collections including *Monday Coffee and Other Stories of Mothering Children with Special Needs*, Where *Mercy and Truth Meet: Homeless Women of Wheeler Speak*, *#keepmuncieweird....and whimsical!* and nine volumes of the *I Remember: Indianapolis Youth Write about Their Lives* series.

Nasreen Khan copy edits for a living and writes poetry to stay sane. She grew up in West Africa and Indonesia and moved to the American Midwest by way of New York City. She lives on Indianapolis's Near Westside. Her Indianapolis writing is all a tribute to Haughville. Walking the streets of Haughville, becoming part of the fabric here has kept her grounded. Haughville has been the backdrop for building community, exploring her queer identity, motherhood, changing careers and teaching her son about race. On a Friday night, she can be found cooking various organ meats or chasing down a stellar mint julep.

Etheridge Knight (1931-1991) was born in Corinth, Mississippi. His family spent a significant portion of Knight's adolescence in Paducah, Kentucky before moving to Indianapolis. While serving an eight-year prison term in the Indiana State Prison, Knight wrote poetry. Renowned poet Gwendolyn Brooks met Knight during a prison visit and encouraged his writing. He published several volumes of poetry, including *Poems from Prison* (Broadside Press, 1968), *Belly Song and Other Poems* (Broadside Press, 1973), which earned both Pulitzer Prize and National Book Award nominations, and *The Essential Etheridge Knight* (University of Pittsburgh Press, 1986). Etheridge Knight died of cancer at the age of 59 and is buried in Crown Hill Cemetery.

Karen Kovacik was Indiana Poet Laureate from 2012-2014. Professor of English at IUPUI, she's the author of the poetry collections *Beyond the Velvet Curtain* and *Metropolis Burning;* the editor of *Scattering the Dark,* an anthology of Polish women poets; and the translator, most recently, of Jacek Dehnel's *Aperture,* a finalist for the 2019 PEN Award for Poetry in Translation. She recently became the cat parent of Gus and Molly.

Elizabeth Krajeck, founding member of the Indiana Writers Center, author of two chapbooks, including *Trigger* (winner of third Indiana chapbook award) and collaborations inspired by visual arts including "Restoration Poetry" based on Creative Renewal project interviews in historic Blue Triangle Residence Hall in Indianapolis; "Half of What We Are Is Broken" an installation at IUPUI's former Cultural Arts Center; "Urban Retail Postcard Poems" with Greg Lucas of the former Lucas Gallery; "The Paint Chip Poems;" and 2018/19 "Poetry in Free Motion" with the Quilt Connection Guild. After retiring from HUD as Indiana's community economic development coordinator for the homeless, Krajeck organized the Artists' Club for children in Dayspring Shelter. Serving as a community liaison for Butler's Center for Citizenship and Community, Krajeck combined service learning with the literary arts. Recent work includes publication in *So It Goes: The Literary Journal of the Kurt Vonnegut Museum and Library*; publication in *Indiana at 200, A Celebration of the Hoosier State*; 2017 summer guest reader at the James Whitcomb Riley Museum; participant in Indy Writers Resist; *True Grit Saloon* reading and publication at the Eiteljorg Museum of American Indian and Western Art; and 2019 publication in Indianapolis Review featuring Indianapolis writers.

Former Indiana Poet Laureate **Norbert Krapf**, a Jasper native, has lived in Indianapolis with his family since 2004. His fourteen poetry collections include the recent *Indiana Hill Country Poems* and *Southwest by Midwest*. He has received a Creative Renewal Fellowship from the Arts Council of Indy and a Glick Indiana Author Award for the body of his work. He has a poem in stained glass at the Indy Airport and Garrison Keillor has read his work on *The Writers Almanac*. He has released a poetry and jazz CD with pianist-composer Monika Herzig and combines poetry and blues with Gordon Bonham.

Anne Laker grew up in Southport and also Hendricks County. A three-time winner of Fountain Square's Masterpiece in a Day poetry contest, she received a Creative Renewal Arts Fellowship in 2016 for her Instagram exhibition project, @10000whens, featuring 30 years of digitized diary entries.

Sarah Layden is the author of *Trip Through Your Wires* (Engine Books), a novel, and *The Story I Tell Myself About Myself*, winner of the Sonder Press Chapbook Competition. Her writing appears in *Boston Review, Salon, The Millions, Blackbird, McSweeney's Internet Tendency*, and elsewhere. She teaches creative writing at Indiana University-Purdue University Indianapolis.

Theon Lee is an Indianapolis-native performance artist, in the fields of Hip Hop (Emcee), Poetry (Spokenword), and folk (vocalist/guitarist/song-writer). Since 2010, Theon has performed to a diverse crowd across the Midwest region and has recently (within the last five years) rooted himself in Teaching Artistry.

Nate Logan is the author of *Inside the Golden Days of Missing You* (Magic Helicopter Press, 2019). He teaches at Marian University.

Jackie Lutzke is a creative nonfiction writer and 10+ year resident of the Irvington neighborhood on Indianapolis's east side. She loves the east side, and Indianapolis, for its simultaneous specificity of place and its every-where-ness.

Ashley L. Mack-Jackson is a native Hoosier and the co-founder of Word As Bond, Inc. (wordasbond.org). She teaches composition and creative writing at Ivy Tech Community College, and her poetry has appeared in literary journals like *Drumvoices Revue* and *Callaloo*.

Kaitlynne Mantooth is a student at Marian University studying English. She plans to pursue a Ph.D. in American Studies. She has lived and served in Indianapolis her entire life and has a love for the people here that stretches beyond the borders of the city. Currently, she lives in a tiny house with her boyfriend, a Husky, and a chinchilla. It's not a wild life but it's a happy one. She hopes to eventually publish a collection of poems.

Michael Martone was born in Fort Wayne. His most recent book is *The Complete Writings of Art Smith, The Bird Boy of Fort Wayne, Edited by Michael Martone.* He lives now in Tuscaloosa.

Chantel Massey is a poet, teaching artist, and avid Anime lover based in Indiana. She is the author of *Bursting at The Seams* (VK Press, 2018). She has received a residency from Wintertangerine and Open Mouth Poetry and a 2019 Best of Net Award nominee. Her work is forthcoming or appears in *FAFCollective, Turnpike Magazine, Indianapolis Contemporary,* and other online and print publications coming elsewhere. Her current focus is on human rights, confessional and emotional honesty about womanhood, identity, sexuality, spirituality, and blackness.

Izera McAfee has an M.A. degree in Philanthropic Studies from Indiana University. She has been a Co-Founder, Executive Director and advisor for numerous nonprofit organizations. Izera is insightful, with interests in women's empowerment and fostering transformation to social justice. She was born in Indianapolis, Indiana and lived in California for many years. Izera found her passion in linking writing, social justice and philanthropy. Her hobbies are cooking, yoga and entrepreneurship adventures.

Michael McColly's essays and journalism have appeared in *The New York Times, The Chicago Tribune, The Sun Magazine,* the online blog *Humans & Nature, NUVO,* and other journals. He is the author of the 2006 Lambda Literary Award-winning memoir, *The After-Death Room: Journey into Spiritual Activism* (Soft Skull Press), which chronicles his journey reporting on AIDS activism in Africa, Asia and America. He has also published *The World Is Round,* which is a collection of college student essays that reflect on immigrating to America. Along with a former student and photographer, Tuong Nguyen, McColly has written and produced a documentary on efforts by social workers in Vietnam who've worked with street youth affected by addiction and infected with HIV/AIDS. He has won a Lisagor Journalism Award, Illinois Arts Council award for Prose, Pen America grants, and fellowships from Yaddo, Blue Mountain Center, Ragdale and MacDowell Colony. He holds a BA degree in Theater and History from Indiana University, MA in Religious Studies from the Divinity School of the University of Chicago, and an MFA in Creative Writing from the University of Washington. He has been a lecturer in Creative Nonfiction in Northwestern's Master's Program in Creative Writing, at Columbia College, and Loyola University. He now teaches creative writing to inmates in Indiana. His present nonfiction focuses on the subject of urban walking and its surprising effects on not only personal health but on public and environmental health as well. In his recent work, he blends environmental reportage, natural history, memoir, as he describes an urban pilgrimage of 65 miles from Chicago along the shore of Lake Michigan through Indiana's heavily industrialized cities to the sand dunes and wetlands of Indiana Dunes National Park. Since 2001 he has been a lecturer in creative nonfiction at Northwestern University's Master's Program in Creative Writing. He has moved back to Indiana to care for his mother who suffers from late-stage Alzheimer's.

Kevin McKelvey is a place-based poet, writer, designer, and social practice artist and works as a Professor and Director of the MA Program in Social Practice Art at University of Indianapolis. He earned an MFA from Southern Illinois University Carbondale and a BA from DePauw University. Recent books include *Dream Wilderness Poems* and *Indiana Nocturnes*, a collaboration with Curtis L. Crisler. He is currently at work on a novel, essays, and other projects. He lives in Indianapolis with his wife and three children surrounded by old-growth beech and maples.

Norman Minnick (editor) is the author of three collections of poetry, *To Taste the Water, Folly,* and a chapbook, *Advice for a Young Poet.* Minnick is the editor of *Between Water and Song: New Poets for the Twenty-First Century* and *Work Toward Knowing: Beginning with Blake* by Jim Watt.

Paul R. Mullins is Professor in the Department of Anthropology at Indiana University-Purdue University Indianapolis (IUPUI) and Docent in Historical Archaeology at the University of Oulu (Finland). His research focuses on the relationship between racism materiality. His work includes *Race and Affluence: An Archaeology of African America and Consumer Culture* (1999) and *Revolting Things: An Archaeology of Shameful Histories and Repulsive Realities* (January 2021).

Lylanne Musselman is an award-winning poet, playwright, and visual artist. Her work has appeared in *Pank, Flying Island, The Tipton Poetry Journal, The New Verse News,* and *The Ekphrastic Review,* among others, and many anthologies. She is the author of five poetry chapbooks, including *Red Mare 16* (Pink House Literary Arts, 2018), a co-author of the volume of poetry, *Company of Women New and Selected Poems* (Chatter House Press, 2013) and a full-length poetry collection, *It's Not Love, Unfortunately* (Chatter House Press, 2018). She has been a Pushcart Prize nominee for her poetry, most recently in 2019.

Susan Neville is the author of six books of creative nonfiction and four short story collections, including her latest, *The Town of Whispering Dolls* from Fiction Collective 2. She teaches at Butler University.

Nicole Poletika is an Indianapolis-based historian, who focuses on social justice and minority history, as well as history relevance. She earned her M.A. in Public History from Indiana University-Indianapolis, along with a Professional Editing Certificate. She is a member of the LGBTQ Indiana Landmarks Committee, advises on several women's suffrage centennial projects, and serves on the Steering Committee of the forthcoming Digital Encyclopedia of Indianapolis. Her work has been featured in Belt Publishing's *The Gary Anthology* and *Dispatches from the Rust Belt, Vol. II: The Best of Belt Magazine 2019.*

Jim Powell earned his MFA in fiction writing from Bowling Green State University in Ohio, briefly ran a bookstore in the LA area, called Liars & Intellectuals, and founded the Writers' Center of Indianapolis (now the Indiana Writers Center) in 1979. As the director of that organization for twenty years, he stopped writing, but a health scare in 2010 pushed him to again make stories. The recipient of a Creative Renewal Fellowship, he produced more than 70 stories, and he offered curmudgeonly but caring mentorship to his students at IUPUI. A collection of his work, *Only Witness,* was published by INwords in 2019. Jim died in Fort Myers Beach, Florida on January 27, 2020.

Nelson Price is an Indianapolis-based author, historian, and journalist. His books include *Indianapolis Then and Now, Indiana Legends: Famous Hoosiers from Johnny Appleseed to David Letterman, The Quiet Hero: A Life of Ryan White, Legendary Hoosiers, So You Think You Know Indiana?,* and

Indianapolis: Leading the Way. A fifth-generation Hoosier, he grew up in Indianapolis and is the host of the radio show "Hoosier History Live" on WICR-FM (88.7). Nelson is a former feature writer and columnist for *The Indianapolis Star.*

Fran Quinn is the author of five books and teaches independent monthly workshops in New York, Philadelphia, Chicago, and Indianapolis.

Nick Reading is the author of *Love & Sundries* (Split Lip Press) and *The Party in Question*, winner of the Burnside Review Chapbook Contest. His work has appeared in many journals including *Twyckenham Notes, Barrow Street, Cincinnati Review, Gulf Coast,* and *jubilat.* He serves as poetry editor for *Sport Literate* and lives in Indianapolis. He also offers workshops through the Indiana Writers Center and the Indiana Humanities Writing Program. For more, visit nickreading.com.

Tatjana Rebelle (they/she) is a mother, activist, organizer, writer, spoken word artist and promoter. They have lived in Indianapolis most of their life, which is where they learned to use their writing to deal with growing up in the Midwest as a non-binary, first-generation Afro-German and Queer person in America.

Stephanie Reid is a writer and an artist who enjoys many creative mediums. This is the first time her writing has been published. The Indianapolis music scene is a major influence on her work.

Jordan Ryan is the Architectural Archivist and coordinates the Indianapolis Bicentennial Collecting Initiative for the Indiana Historical Society Archives & Library. They have a master's degree in Public History from IUPUI and a bachelor's degree in Art History from Herron School of Art & Design. Their scholarship revolves around the urban built environment, historic preservation, redlining, highway displacement, hostile architecture, and LGBTQ historic sites.

Dr. Sandy Eisenberg Sasso is Rabbi Emerita of Congregation Beth-El Zedeck, where she served for 36 years from 1977-2013. She is currently Director of the Religion, Spirituality and the Arts Initiative at IUPUI Arts and Humanities. In 2016 she co-founded of Women4Change Indiana and is active in the civic and interfaith community. Dr. Sasso has edited books on spirituality and storytelling and authored many award-winning children's books. She is the 2018 recipient of the Eugene and Marilyn Glick Author's Award. She lectures on feminism, children's spirituality, Biblical narrative and the arts. She received her B.A. and M.A. from Temple University and, in 1974, became the first woman ordained a Rabbi from the Reconstructionist Rabbinical College. She earned her Doctorate of Ministry from Christian Theological Seminary in 1996. She and her husband, Dr. Dennis Sasso were the first practicing rabbinical couple in Jewish history.

Barbara Shoup is the author of eight novels for adults and young adults, most recently *An American Tune* and *Looking for Jack Kerouac*, and two books about writing, *A Commotion in Your Heart: Notes about Writing and Life* and *Novel Ideas: Contemporary Authors Share the Creative Process.* Her creative nonfiction has been published lately in *Atticus, Ocotillo Review,* and *Another Chicago Magazine.* She is the Writer-in-Residence at the Indiana Writers Center and a faculty member at Art Workshop International.

Natalie Solmer grew up in South Bend, Indiana. She is the founder and Editor-in-Chief of *The Indianapolis Review*, an online journal of poetry and art. She worked as a floral department manager at Marsh Supermarkets for 13 years, and now teaches composition and writing at Ivy Tech Community College in Indianapolis. Her work has been published in journals such as *Willow Springs, North American Review, Briar Cliff Review, Pleiades,* and forthcoming from *Colorado Review.*

Chris Speckman teaches at Butler University and Shortridge High School. His work has appeared in *Scoundrel Time, Cimarron Review, Passages North, PANK,* and the anthology *It Was Written: Poetry Inspired by Hip-Hop.*

Ruth Stone (1915-2011) grew up in Indianapolis, the daughter of Roger McDowell Perkins, a typesetter for the *Indianapolis Star* and part-time drummer, and Ruth Ferguson Perkins, who loved to recite Tennyson out loud while nursing her daughter. Her books of poetry include *In the Next Galaxy* (2002), *In the Dark* (2004), and *Ordinary Words* (1999). Stone taught creative writing at many universities while making her home base in Vermont, finally tenuring at SUNY Binghamton. Her farmhouse in Goshen, VT is now the site of a literary nonprofit, The Ruth Stone House, committed to preserving her life and legacy and creating a space for artists and writers to teach, learn and create new work.

Grant Vecera's poems have appeared in such magazines as *Louisiana Literature, Concho River Review, Chiron Review, Birmingham Poetry Review, Green Hills Literary Lantern, Southern Indiana Review*, and many others. He lives in Indianapolis with his lovely wife, hilarious daughter, and various animal companions.

Manòn Voice is a native of Indianapolis and is a poet and writer, spoken word artist, hip-hop emcee, educator, social justice advocate, community builder and practicing contemplative. Manòn Voice is a Pushcart Prize in Poetry nominee and is also a recipient of the 2020 Robert D. Beckmann Jr., Emerging Artist Fellowship from the Arts Council of Indianapolis. She considers much of her work to be poetic documentaries exploring the intersections of our past, present and future selves while illuminating the possibilities of our astounding human capacity and potential.

Shari Wagner, a former Indiana Poet Laureate, is the author of three books of poems: *The Farm Wife's Almanac, The Harmonist at Nightfall: Poems of Indiana,* and *Evening Chore.* She has an MFA in Creative Writing from Indiana University and teaches for the Indiana Writers Center, Bethany Seminary, and IUPUI's Religion, Spirituality and the Arts Initiative. Her poems have appeared in *American Life in Poetry, The Writer's Almanac, North American Review,* and *Shenandoah.*

Dan Wakefield is a novelist, journalist and screenwriter. His books include the novel *Going All the Way,* and the memoir *New York in the Fifties.*

PERMISSIONS

Desiree Arce: "International Oasis in the Midwest." Copyright © Desiree Arce. Used by permission of the author.

Michael Brockley: "Hawking Indy 500 Souvenirs During the 100th Running of the Greatest Spectacle in Racing." Copyright © Michael Brockley. Used by permission of the author.

A'Lelia Bundles: "The Story Behind Telling Madam C. J. Walker's Story." Copyright © A'Lelia Bundles. Used by permission of the author.

Dan Carpenter: "Mourning at the Mlk-Rfk Memorial." Copyright © Dan Carpenter. Used by permission of the author.

Jared Carter: "Back Home Again in Indy" from *Urban Voices: 51 Poems from 51 American Poets.* Copyright © 2014 by Jared Carter. Used by permission of the author.

Malachi Carter: "Downtown, Anywhere" first published in *The Indianapolis Review,* Issue 10: Fall 2019. Copyright © Malachi Carter. Used by permission of the author.

Bryan Furuness: "Find Your Own." Copyright © Bryan Furuness. Used by permission of the author.

Dan Grossman: "Soldiers and Sailors Monument, Indianapolis." Copyright © Dan Grossman. Used by permission of the author.

Terrance Hayes: "What Was the Contribution of Neighbors? from *To Float in the Space Between: A Life and Work in Conversation with the Life and Work of Etheridge Knight.* Copyright 2018 © Terrance Hayes. Reprinted with permission of the author and Wave Books.

Will Higgins: "Pink Pony." Copyright © Will Higgins. Used by permission of the author.

Susan Neville: "Birds of Prey." Copyright © Susan Neville. Used by permission of the author.

Nicole Poletika: "'Moral Warfare:' Indianapolis Women's Long-Fought Battle for the Vote." Copyright © Nicole Poletika. Used by permission of the author.

Jim Powell: "Puppies 4 Sale" from *Only Witness*. Copyright © 2019 by Jim Powell. Published by INWords. Used by permission.

Nelson Price: "Doc Coe and the Malaria Epidemic." Copyright © Nelson Price. Used by permission of the author.

Fran Quinn: "Indianapolis" from *The Horse of Blue Ink*. Copyright © 2005 by Fran Quinn. Published by Blue Sofa Press. Used by permission.

Nick Reading: "Jazz Kitchen." Originally published in *Painted Bride Quarterly*, Issue 77. Copyright © Nick Reading. Used by permission of the author.

Tatjana Rebelle: "Through Our Eyes." Originally published by CCIF. Copyright © Tatjana Rebelle. Used by permission of the author.

Stephanie Reid: "Punk Rock in Naptown." Copyright © Stephanie Reid. Used by permission of the author.

Jordan B. Ryan: "Imagining the Black Crossroads: Music and Memory on Indiana Avenue." Copyright © Paul R. Mullins and Jordan B. Ryan. Used by permission of the authors.

Sandy Eisenberg Sasso: "State Museum Thoughts." *Heritage Keepers Award, 2014*. Copyright © Sandy Eisenberg Sasso. Used by permission of the author.

Barbara Shoup: "Our House." Copyright © Barbara Shoup. Used by permission of the author.

Natalie Solmer: "Floral Lady's Employer Files for Bankruptcy." Copyright © Natalie Solmer. Used by permission of the author.